AUSTSWIM

Teaching Swimming and Water Safety
The Australian Way

Contributors

John Harmer   John Kilpatrick

Sarie Lowden   Jenni Maclean

Kirk Marks   Peter Meaney

Ken Richter   Julie Tullberg

David White

Illustrated by
Mary Ann Hurley and Azoo Design

Library of Congress Cataloging-in-Publication Data

Teaching swimming and water safety: the Australian way / contributing authors John Harmer, Sarie Lowden, Kirk Marks ... [et al.].; illustrated by Mary Ann Hurley and Azoo Design.

    p. cm.

    At head of title: AUSTSWIM.

    ISBN 0-7360-3251-7

    1. Swimming for children--Study and teaching--Australia. 2. Aquatic sports--Safety measures. I. Harmer, John. II. Lowden, Sarie. III. Marks, Kirk. IV. AUSTSWIM Inc.

GV837.2.T42 2000

797.2'0028'9--dc21

                         00-044937

ISBN: 0-7360-3251-7

This book is a revised edition of *Teaching Swimming and Water Safety: The Australian Way,* published in 1998 by AUSTSWIM Inc.

Managing Editors: Leigh LaHood and Laurie Stokoe; **Proofreader:** Erin Cler; **Graphic Designer:** Nancy Rasmus; **Graphic Artists:** Amy Markstahler and Brian McElwain; **Cover Designer:** Jack W. Davis; **Photographer and Illustrator:** Mary Ann Hurley and Azoo Design; **Printer:** United Graphics

Human Kinetics books are available at special discounts for bulk purchase. Special editions or book excerpts can also be created to specification. For details, contact the Special Sales Manager at Human Kinetics.

Printed in the United States of America

10 9 8 7 6 5 4 3 2 1

Human Kinetics
Web site: www.humankinetics.com

United States: Human Kinetics
P.O. Box 5076
Champaign, IL 61825-5076
800-747-4457
e-mail: humank@hkusa.com

Canada: Human Kinetics
475 Devonshire Road Unit 100
Windsor, ON N8Y 2L5
800-465-7301 (in Canada only)
e-mail: hkcan@mnsi.net

Europe: Human Kinetics
P.O. Box IW14
Leeds LS16 6TR, United Kingdom
+44 (0)113 278 1708
e-mail: humank@hkeurope.com

Australia: Human Kinetics
57A Price Avenue
Lower Mitcham, South Australia 5062
08 8277 1555
e-mail: liahka@senet.com.au

New Zealand: Human Kinetics
P.O. Box 105-231, Auckland Central
09-309-1890
e-mail: hkp@ihug.co.nz

To dream anything that you want to dream. That is the beauty
of the human will. To do anything that you want to do. That is the
strength of the human will. To trust yourself to test your limits.
That is the courage to succeed.

Bernard Edmonds
American writer

(*quoted in* Commitment to Excellence, Great Quotations, *1985*)

CONTENTS

FOREWORD

AUSTSWIM has gained an outstanding reputation for the training of swimming and water safety teachers. AUSTSWIM teaching awards are recognised by the government and the aquatic industry as the yardstick for competency-based training in the field. The manual has been designed to assist course candidates to acquire the appropriate knowledge and skill to become competent teachers of swimming and water safety.

This manual covers topics deemed necessary for teaching water familiarisation, floating and movement, entries and a range of swimming strokes. While skills are being developed, every opportunity is taken to impart water safety knowledge to reduce the likelihood of aquatic accidents, including drownings.

This manual plays an important role in facilitating the delivery of quality learn-to-swim programs throughout Australia.

I am impressed with the quality of the AUSTSWIM text; this book will confidently take AUSTSWIM into the new millenium with a further outstanding resource. The book will provide many swimming teachers and instructors with a valuable resource and can also be used as a reference again and again.

The easy-to-use format and the teaching hints and processes will ensure that many teachers, instructors or students will find that many questions that they may have are answered; they can be assured that the information is up to date and world leading.

AUSTSWIM is dedicated to developing the most up-to-date swimming teaching resources and will continue with the commitment to ensure that they remain at the forefront of swimming teaching today.

Kirk Marks
Chairman
September 1999

PUBLISHER'S PREFACE

The swimming programs developed by the Australian aquatics organisation AUSTSWIM are known throughout the world for their excellence. Those in the field of aquatics also recognise AUSTSWIM's instructor training for these successful programs as the yardstick for competency-based training. Human Kinetics is proud to offer this international edition of the AUSTSWIM manual *Teaching Swimming and Water Safety*. Now instructor candidates everywhere can study it to develop the knowledge and skills they need to become proficient teachers of swimming and water safety.

The manual begins with the essentials of water safety, including hypothermia, survival in the water, safe behaviour in the water, preparations for safe aquatics programs, and emergency procedures. It next turns to water familiarisation, covering topics such as water entries and exits, the use of aids and equipment with beginners, getting the face wet and submerging, moving through the water and returning to a standing position, breathing in the water, and safety and basic rescue skills. Chapter 3 discusses floating and movement in the water, with sections on water safety activities, introduction to the deep water, and games. Chapter 4 explains how to apply physics principles to movement in the water, while chapter 5 provides methods for introducing students to diving. The last chapter contains detailed descriptions of how to perform correctly six common strokes: freestyle, backstroke, breaststroke, butterfly, sidestroke, and survival backstroke.

Teaching Swimming and Water Safety is an outstanding resource that instructors can refer to again and again. Its easy-to-use format and the teaching hints and processes it includes will answer many instructors' and students' questions. Instructors can rely on this manual for the useful, up-to-date information they need.

ACKNOWLEDGMENTS

AUSTSWIM gratefully acknowledges the generous support provided by the Commonwealth Government through the National Office of Sport and Recreation Policy of the Department of Industry, Science and Tourism.

Chapter 1

SAFETY ESSENTIALS

Water Safety

Adults placed in a position of authority have a 'Duty of Care' to those in their charge. Employers are responsible for ensuring that the teachers whom they employ are competent in the essential rescue skills that are appropriate for the environment in which they are teaching.

This chapter aims to provide essential water safety knowledge that may be an integral part of a swimming program and rescue skills that may be required by teachers. Safety is the highest priority in any aquatic activity. This chapter will assist teachers to conduct all lessons safely.

Water safety is an essential component of every aquatics program. For most children, water safety education begins at home in the very early years. It is important that this education should continue throughout the aquatics program.

The aim of water safety education is to enable students to recognise and assess potential aquatic dangers and to develop a realistic understanding of their swimming ability in various water and weather conditions. The practice of water safety, lifesaving and survival skills should commence early in the aquatic program within the constraints of the pool environment. As confidence and ability increase, these skills should be practised in open water if at all possible. The students will develop confidence, competence, endurance and judgement skills that should maximise the chance of survival in an emergency.

Water safety education is primarily concerned with the prevention of drowning. By using the skills learned in the program and by acknowledging the importance of self-preservation, students should be able to avoid life-threatening situations. However, some emergency incidents are not predictable, and the ability to make a calm assessment and to perform survival skills suitable to the particular conditions is essential.

The majority of drownings occur in inland waters, although a significant number occur in the sea. Statistics indicate that

- 80 per cent of those who drown are male;
- 40 per cent of those who drown are children under 18 years; and
- 70 per cent of drownings occur within 20 metres (65.5 feet) of safety.

Water Movement

Sea, river and lake environments all have water movement to varying degrees. This movement may change in direction and strength and is potentially dangerous for those who are unaware of its effects.

Moving water can increase the hazards of the following:

- Potholes
- Submerged objects
- Crumbling banks and cliffs
- Submerged tree trunks
- Overhanging branches
- Sandbars

Potholes.

Submerged objects.

Weeds

Weeds may occur in all environments and should be avoided whenever possible. If caught in weeds or kelp, swimmers should

- remain calm,
- use a restricted breaststroke arm action,
- trail their legs while their arms move the body out of the weeds, and
- swim slowly.

If tangled in the weeds, swimmers should remain calm, keep all movements to a minimum and remove the weeds before swimming out.

Crumbling banks and cliffs.

Cold Water and Immersion Hypothermia

Hypothermia occurs when the body core temperature (particularly of the heart, lungs and brain) falls. Immersion hypothermia is an acute type of hypothermia produced when a person is immersed in cold water.

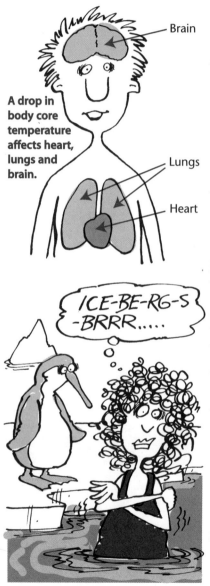

A drop in body core temperature affects heart, lungs and brain.

Brain

Lungs

Heart

Violent shivering.

Normal body core temperature in a healthy person is about 36.9°C (98°F). This level is constant and is necessary for heart, lungs and brain function. Maintaining the core temperature at this constant level is a function of a special section of the brain that is sensitive to small changes in deep core temperature. This section also monitors superficial temperature receptors.

Under normal conditions, the body copes well with exposure to cold or heat. However, when the difference in temperature between the cold environment and the normal body temperature is too great, heat loss exceeds heat production, the thermo-regulating mechanism fails and the body core cools. This occurs in water temperatures of 20°C (68°F) and below.

When exposed to cold conditions the body reacts as follows:

At body temperatures of 37°C-35°C (99°F-95°F)

- Intense and uncontrollable shivering

- Impaired performance of complex tasks

At body temperatures of 35°C-33°C (95°F-91°F)

- Violent shivering

- Difficulty in speaking

At body temperatures of 33°C-30°C (91°F-86°F)

- Decreased shivering replaced by muscular rigidity
- Reduced muscle coordination, producing erratic or jerky movements
- Maintenance of posture and appearance of coherence in most cases
- Cloudy thinking, lessened general comprehension of the situation, possible amnesia

At body temperatures of 30°C to 27°C (86°F-81°F)

- Unconsciousness
- No response to the spoken word
- No functioning of most reflexes
- Heartbeat erratic

At body temperatures below 25°C (77°F)

- Failure of cardiac and respiratory centers in the brain
- Probable oedema (edema) and haemorrhage (hemorrhage) on the lungs
- Death

Survival Time

Survival time varies according to age, gender, body size and weight. The figures in the survival chart apply to an adult of average size–approximately 70 kilograms (154 pounds). The survival time is tabulated according to water temperature.

Temperature (°C)	Survival time (hours)
9.5	2-3
11.0	4
12.0	4-5
14.0	6
16.0	7-8
18.0	10

Wind Chill

Wind has an important effect on the temperature felt. The body cools itself by several methods, including radiation, respiration, evaporation, condensation and convection. The colder the air temperature, the greater the heat loss from the body.

The body warms a thin layer of air around it, and if this layer is blown away, a higher rate of heat loss occurs and the body feels colder. The wind chill diagram gives an idea of the magnitude of this effect.

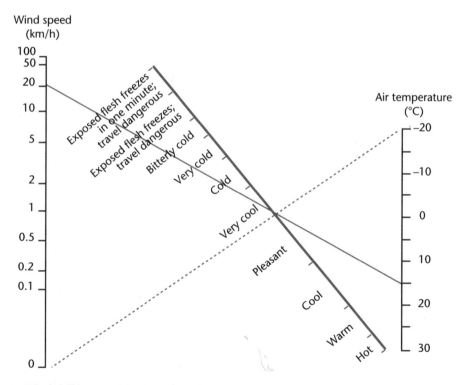

Wind chill is a combination of wind speed and air temperature.

Cold Water Survival

A person who is unexpectedly immersed in cold water should not remove any clothing, except for a heavy item such as an overcoat.

A person wearing a flotation device can increase survival time by assuming the Heat Escape Lessening Position (HELP). The knees are bent and drawn towards the chest, and the arms are pressed firmly against the sides of the chest. This position delays heat loss by protecting the most vulnerable areas: the head, the sides of the chest and the groin.

The Heat Escape Lessening Position.

In rough, cold water, an average swimmer without a flotation device should not swim a distance greater than one-tenth of his or her swimming ability. If the swimmer is close to the wreckage of a craft, he or she should attempt to climb onto the vessel and should maintain warmth by tucking into a ball.

The 'huddle' position is based on the same principle as the HELP and was developed for groups of three or more people. The sides of the chest, the groin and the lower body are pressed together. This formation is particularly useful if small children are involved, as they can be supported, protected and warmed in the centre of the group.

The huddle.

If swimmers must stay in deep water without a flotation device for a long period, they should remain as still as possible, conserving energy and, if possible, staying in a tucked position. They should maintain this position through slow sculling of the hands. As the body's core temperature drops, it will become increasingly difficult for swimmers to make sensible decisions. Purposeful muscle movements (e.g. swimming or holding onto a boat) become difficult, and people may be unaware of their plight.

Treatment of Hypothermia

The hypothermia victim must always be handled very gently and rewarmed slowly. If the victim is conscious, do the following:

- Remove the victim from the water.
- Shelter him or her from the wind and rain immediately.
- Create a sheltered, warm, dry place.
- Remove the victim's wet clothing and wrap the victim in blankets, space blankets or a sleeping bag.
- Huddle together for warmth so body temperature can rise gradually.
- Give the victim warm, sweet drinks.
- Seek medical aid.

Do not do any of the following:

- Apply excessive external heat (e.g. fire or an electric blanket) to the victim's body.
- Massage the victim's arms and legs.
- Give the victim alcohol.
- Move the victim.

If the victim is unconscious, follow the usual procedure for maintaining breathing and circulation at all times during treatment.

Survival in the Water

Most people learn to swim so that they can enjoy a wide variety of aquatic activities. As competence and skill increase, swimmers progress to aquatic environments in which the margin of safety is reduced.

Each emergency is different, and therefore the skills required to perform the required action will vary.

Swimmers must have a realistic understanding of their personal abilities, the knowledge to assess the situation and form a workable plan of action and the capability to perform survival skills.

Personal survival education should provide students with these elements:

- Knowledge of the specific dangers in each aquatic environment
- Skill in applying a wide range of survival techniques
- The ability to select and perform the most suitable survival procedures
- The ability to improvise in the use of aids
- The capacity for endurance and skill in the water

When assessing an emergency, swimmers should consider these factors:

- The distance from safety
- The weather and water conditions
- The availability of flotation aids
- The removal or retention of any articles of clothing
- The chances of reaching safety

These considerations should provide sufficient information for an appropriate plan of action.

If entry to the water is unavoidable, the swimmer's first action may be to obtain a flotation aid. Donning a personal flotation device (PFD) prior to entry may assist survival. Next, a safe method of entry must be selected. Once in the water, the swimmer must employ the skill most suitable in the prevailing conditions. However, conditions may change quickly, so a person in a survival predicament may have to adapt both skills and a plan of action quickly. When the swimmer reaches safety, he or she must evaluate whether to seek help from others or medical intervention and how to report the incident to appropriate authorities.

Safe Behaviour

Swimming Alone

Many drownings could be avoided if people observed the 'never swim alone' rule. People should undertake aquatic activities in the company of others, preferably those skilled in rescue and resuscitation techniques.

Use of Aids

Flotation aids must be checked before and after use, and faulty or damaged aids must be repaired immediately. Average swimmers should not depend on buoyant toys to keep them afloat in deep water. Aids should not be used in strong winds or currents or in crowded swimming areas.

Suitable Clothing

People should choose clothing suitable for expected conditions and activities. They should tie back long hair and remove jewellery. Those who are boating should wear PFDs and non-skid footwear.

Distance Estimation

Distance across water is very difficult to estimate accurately, the usual error being underestimation. Distance may be increased by the effects of currents and wind.

Depth of Water

Extreme caution must be exercised when entering water for which the depth is unknown. A dive entry in shallow water may result in a spinal cord injury. Diving entries should take place only in deep water in controlled swimming environments where the person has the appropriate diving skill. AUSTSWIM defines shallow water as 'water below the extended arms'. Where there are waves, the crest of the wave should be used as the water level.

Using a PFD.

Preparing and Planning a Safe Aquatics Program

The Swimming Area

The swimming area should be checked for depth, holes, snags, currents, slippery rocks or tiles or any other likely hazard. In pools or other limited spaces, an area should be designated for beginners. A handy aid for defining areas in pools and open water is a collection of plastic fruit juice containers tied to a weight or tied to a floating rope and anchored at corner points. The containers can be positioned to define the teaching area limits for the class. In natural aquatic environments, floats of distinctive colours can be used to denote potential hazards that cannot be eliminated.

Open water swimming area.

Secure Rest Stations

Secure rest stations, which may also be used in emergency situations, must be placed in selected areas. Tyre tubes firmly lashed together and anchored to the bottom will suffice if permanent pontoons are not available.

Rest station.

Rescue Craft

A maneuverable and quick rescue craft is essential at natural water locations, even if the water is shallow. A stable craft such as a surf rescue board also provides a rest station and forms an excellent teaching platform, allowing the teacher to maintain a clear view of the class.

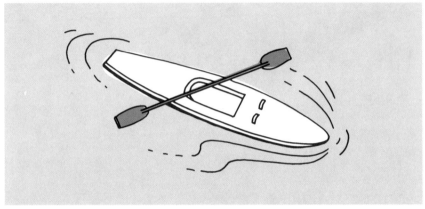

Rescue craft.

River Location

At a river location the teacher should remain on the down-current side of the group wherever possible. Catch ropes, placed across the current downstream from the working area, may be grasped in an emergency.

Safety Behaviour

Information about emergency procedures and dangerous places, conditions and behaviours (e.g. pushing in) should be provided, and its importance emphasised, from the outset. Students should never dive or jump in the water at the beginning of a lesson but rather sit down and slide in.

Medical History

The medical history of all students should be known, particularly in regard to epilepsy, heart disease and asthma. Every time a student enrols, a section on medical history should be completed for the teacher's record.

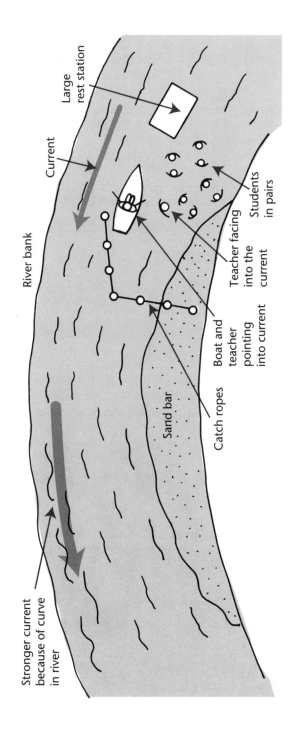

Large
rest station

Current

River bank

Stronger current
because of curve
in river

Sand bar

Catch ropes

Boat and
teacher
pointing
into current

Teacher facing
into the
current

Students
in pairs

Teaching station in a flowing river.

15

Buddies.

Staying in Pairs

In large groups, everyone should have a 'buddy'. If there is a spare person, have one threesome. The teacher should not act as a buddy.

Behaviour in Emergencies

Emergency procedures should be practised even though it is hoped an emergency will never arise. Don't assume that emergencies will never happen!

Lifesaving and Resuscitation

Lifesaving and resuscitation skills are often neglected. It is the responsibility of teachers to hold current qualifications or certifications.

The Class

The class is the teacher's responsibility. In an emergency, teachers must not leave the class alone. If necessary, another teacher should take control of two classes temporarily, with the students out of the water.

Don't leave the class alone.

Check the roll.

The teacher should check the roll at the beginning and end of each lesson and do 'head counts' during lessons, particularly when classes are large and conditions crowded.

Temperature Extremes

Extremes of temperature, either heat or cold, can be dangerous to some people and are uncomfortable for all. Long periods in direct sun or cold winds should be avoided unless students are suitably dressed.

Skin Care

Exposure to the sun's ultraviolet rays is the main cause of skin cancer. The most dangerous years are during childhood. Exposure to the sun during these years considerably increases the likelihood of skin cancer later in life.

Everyone is at risk, but a fair-skinned person who does not tan but reddens in the sun is at greatest risk. People with red hair or blue eyes and those who freckle or have many moles face a higher risk of developing skin cancer.

Reduce the risk by doing the following:

- Avoid the sun in the middle of the day (11 A.M. to 3 P.M. daylight saving time).

- Wear protective clothing such as a wide-brimmed hat and a long-sleeved shirt.

- Use maximum protection sunscreen (SPF 15+ broad spectrum) on skin which cannot be covered with clothes.

- Stay in the shade when possible.

Wear protective clothing.

Teachers should ensure that children are well protected. Teachers must encourage students to observe these safe practices when classes are conducted in the open.

Box Jellyfish

The lethal box jellyfish is prevalent in tropical and sub-tropical waters north of the Tropic of Capricorn. It may be found all year-round, but is particularly widespread between October and May. It can sting even in shallow water, when people are launching boats or just paddling on the beach. Swimmers should wear protective clothing (i.e. a stinger suit) if they must enter the water.

Sting symptoms are immediate and increasing pain and red or purple weals on the skin. Whitish strings will also be seen adhering to the skin.

If a swimmer is stung, do the following:

- Retrieve the victim from the water.
- Position the victim with the head lower than the body.
- Commence Expired Air Resuscitation (EAR) or Cardio-pulmonary Resuscitation (CPR) if necessary.
- Douse tentacles liberally with vinegar.
- Send for medical assistance.
- If the victim is unconscious, monitor breathing and pulse.

Do not attempt to remove the tentacles or rub with sand.

Class Safety and Emergency Procedures

The safety of students in a class must be the primary consideration of teachers at all times. In agreeing to teach students, whether in a paid or voluntary capacity, teachers are always responsible for the safety of the group. They are said to be 'in loco parentis' (in place of the parent).

At some swimming locations, additional safety support may be provided, such as qualified pool attendants or lifeguards. Irrespective of such support being available, ultimate responsibility for the safety of groups being taught falls on the swimming

Class safety.

teachers. It is therefore essential that teachers have developed an emergency plan and have been well versed in safety procedures, rescue and follow-up procedures.

The majority of swimming pool complexes have established, well-documented emergency procedures. Teachers using these pools must thoroughly familiarise themselves with the emergency procedures being practised at those pools.

Developing an Emergency Plan

One of the first tasks in the development of an emergency procedure is the establishment of an aquatic environment checklist. The development of a checklist will indicate if the facility has the appropriate equipment for an emergency.

Thorough preparation is essential to ensure the smooth and efficient mobilisation of an emergency plan. Swimming teachers need to carefully plan emergency procedures and maintain a checklist of updated, essential information, which should be displayed prominently in the swimming area.

Aquatic Environment Checklist

Name of aquatic environment _____ Manager _____

Address _____ Teacher _____

_____ Postcode _____ in charge

Type of environment

Indoor ❏

Outdoor ❏

Heated ❏

Open water—ocean ❏

Open water—lake ❏

Open water—river ❏

Emergency equipment

First aid room ❏

First aid kit ❏

Resuscitator ❏

Spinal injury board ❏

Emergency procedures ❏

Plan ❏

Teaching equipment

Comments

Name _____ Date _____

The points in the box on page 21 must be considered in developing a checklist.

It is disturbing in an emergency situation to discover that the telephone is locked away during lunchtime and nobody knows where to find the key, or that the cupboard has been cleaned and the first aid kit has been removed. Access to emergency equipment, particularly a telephone with a direct line, must be maintained at all times.

Swimming teachers working in natural water environments have to be particularly well prepared for emergency situations. Communication and immediate access to assistance have to be carefully and thoroughly considered and an emergency plan specifically developed for the working area.

In determining emergency procedures, teachers must consider the minimum number of competent people required should an emergency situation arise. Consideration should be given to who performs the following functions:

- Leaving to get assistance
- Looking after the class(es)
- Performing the 'rescue' (if necessary)
- Administering first aid

Emergency Checklist

- ☐ Location of nearest telephone

  – Is it always accessible?

- ☐ Location and telephone number of nearest ambulance

- ☐ Location and telephone number of nearest medical assistance (if ambulance is not readily available)

- ☐ Means of transport to medical assistance

- ☐ Location of first aid kit

  – Is it always accessible?

  – Is it always unlocked?

  – Is it well stocked?

- ☐ Location of rescue equipment (eg ropes, poles, rescue tubes, kickboards)

- ☐ Names of first aid personnel on site

- ☐ Emergency signal to be used

  – bell

  – whistle (including the number of times sound is heard, e.g. one long whistle)

  – siren

- ☐ Statement of emergency procedures to be implemented

  – emergency action

  – role of staff involved

  – follow-up procedures

- ☐ Supplementary list of other helpful agencies (e.g. first aid, fire brigade or department, poison information bureau or centre)

Here is an example of the actions that might be planned for three people:

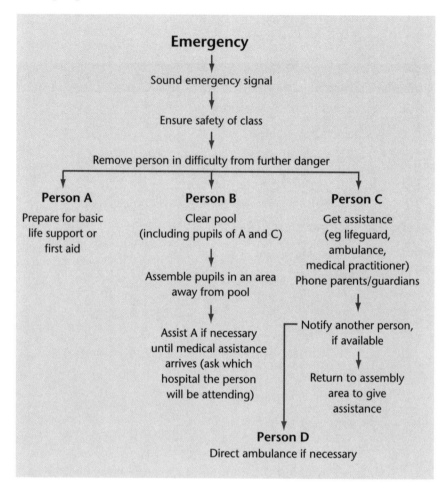

Emergency

↓

Sound emergency signal

↓

Ensure safety of class

↓

Remove person in difficulty from further danger

Person A

Prepare for basic life support or first aid

Person B

Clear pool (including pupils of A and C)

↓

Assemble pupils in an area away from pool

↓

Assist A if necessary until medical assistance arrives (ask which hospital the person will be attending)

Person C

Get assistance (eg lifeguard, ambulance, medical practitioner) Phone parents/guardians

↓

Notify another person, if available

↓

Return to assembly area to give assistance

Person D

Direct ambulance if necessary

Everyone involved in a swimming program must know his or her role should an emergency situation arise. This will ensure the smooth and efficient implementation of emergency actions and avoid indecision and replication of tasks.

Often emergency procedures look great on paper but flaws are discovered during an accident. Obviously, for any plan to operate efficiently, it must be practised regularly. Emergency drills will only operate effectively if all teachers at a swimming area, plus the staff and pool manager (if applicable), have discussed and become familiar with their respective roles. If the practice sessions do not work smoothly at first, further practice sessions will be necessary until they do. If the practices continue to be unsuccessful, an alternative plan must be considered. Emergency drills are important. They should not be seen as a break from lessons, a joke or a game.

Qualifications (Certifications)

Swimming teachers must maintain current swimming, rescue, resuscitation and first aid qualifications or certifications. Teachers instructing in open water are required to hold the relevant rescue qualification or certification for the environment in which they are teaching.

After an Emergency

Teachers must be familiar with the actions required by their class organisers or employers immediately following an accident. This might involve providing information to the following people or groups:

- Pool manager
- Local council
- School principal
- State or regional office
- Education department

In all cases a detailed accident report needs to be completed and signed by competent witnesses (particularly those directly involved). Details of times and actions taken are very important. Remember that legal action often takes years to come to court. It will be very difficult for teachers to recall exactly what occurred years previously!

.

AU**S**TSWIM.

Chapter 2

BECOMING FAMILIAR WITH THE WATER

Aims of the Swimming and Water Safety Program

Ideally, the first contact that beginning swimmers have with the water should be an active, enjoyable and fun experience. Carefully graduated progressions which reinforce positive experiences should be developed by swimming teachers.

The swimming program has these aims:

- To encourage the development of beginners' confidence in the water by providing a wide variety of activities in safe environments
- To increase students' awareness and understanding of the need for water safety by teaching the appropriate knowledge, skills and activities
- To encourage the development of swimming strokes and other water skills which form the basis of recreational swimming and aquatic activities
- To encourage the development of lifesaving skills

The initial stages cannot be rushed. Beginners must be able to progress at their own pace and according to their own abilities. They should be given time to explore what their bodies can and cannot do.

It is essential that teachers understand the needs and fears of each beginner. Teachers should offer reassurance and encouragement and sense when beginners are apprehensive about a particular activity. If beginners are reticent to attempt something new, teachers should recognise the need to take a step back and reintroduce the activity via another approach.

Beginning swimmers constantly challenge their teachers. For the teachers, this stage can provide one of the most rewarding times in teaching swimming. Few things can rival the satisfaction of observing reticent beginners develop into happy 'water babies' eager for their next swimming lesson.

Force has no place in the teaching of swimming. Positive feedback is the best method of reinforcing the development of skills. Praise works wonders in forming good habits and motivating beginners.

Beginners must have confidence in their ability to attempt an activity. The success of teachers involved in teaching beginners should be measured by the confidence levels and overall happiness of their students.

Without trust, there is fear and little enjoyment; without enjoyment, there will be little practice; and without practice, beginners will not consolidate the skills or develop the positive attitudes required to learn how to swim.

Beginners are all different.

Fun activities and games are essential in learning. Beginners, young or old, will achieve more through fun than fear. Through fun games and activities, skills can be introduced without beginners even realising; their attention is more on the activity than on their possible fear of the water.

The three initial skills beginners must acquire before further skills are introduced are these:

- Water familiarisation
- Buoyancy
- Mobility

Movement through these skill stages is like a chain, with each link closely connected to the others. Progression through these stages should be with encouragement, praise and understanding from the teachers.

As the beginners develop confidence in the water and gain trust in their teachers, deep water activities can be introduced. Taken slowly and with lots of encouragement, teachers can help beginners to become accustomed to deep water. As the beginners' confidence grows, deep water skills can be introduced.

Needs of Beginners

Beginners need teachers who have good teaching skills and who are friendly and consistent. Other factors that are important for beginners are the following:

- Comfortable water temperature

- Clear, clean water

- Familiar surroundings (e.g. location of deep water, toilets, entry and exit points)

- Knowledge and understanding of the safety regulations

- Defined working areas

- A friendly working atmosphere

- Success within the lesson

- Working with others of similar ability

- Correct use of swimming aids

- Working areas free of distractions

- A 'dry activities' area for out-of-water activities (e.g. on cold days)

Beginners need security.

Equipment for Beginners

Here are the types of equipment that teachers can use to make lessons fun and enjoyable:

- Kickboards
- Swim wings
- Bubbles
- Animal kickboards
- Swim belts
- Small buckets

- Water mats
- PFDs
- Swim rings
- Dive rings
- Hand dumbbells
- Water toys
- Broom handles
- Barbells
- Balls
- Hoops
- Toys

Teachers should use the equipment as working aids so beginners, through play activities, learn to become relaxed and mobile. Most importantly, beginners need teachers with imagination and enthusiasm.

Equipment for beginners.

Use of Aids

Aids can be extremely useful and enable beginners to practise a desired skill with less fatigue. Teachers should be prepared to patiently lead students through a range of progressive activities supplemented with incidental use of a variety of equipment. This will gradually increase students' understanding and recognition that the water will support them, with or without other artificial support.

With timid or awkward students, flotation aids such as floats and bubbles may help them obtain sufficient control and balance to maintain a buoyant position. The use of different flotation aids is important, but dependence on them should be reduced systematically and eliminated as soon as possible.

For beginners, becoming familiar with water is a whole new environmental experience. Teachers should not expect beginners to arrive for the lesson knowing and understanding Bernoulli's, Archimedes's or Newton's set of principles. Beginners, on entering the water, experience firsthand how their bodies are affected by water. They discover for themselves that

- walking requires more effort;
- falling over is like falling in 'slow motion';
- it is more difficult to regain their balance when they fall over;
- they experience a feeling of heaviness around the chest and a restriction in breathing when they wade into deeper water; and
- they experience sensations of semi-weightlessness.

Beginners must not only become familiar with the water and their new surroundings but also with other children and adults who are initially strangers to them. They may feel very anxious about entering the water but equally concerned about being left with teachers who are foreign to them. Teachers must understand these concerns and exercise care and patience in helping beginners to adjust to this new environment.

Solutions to Beginners' Problems

In the following table are some of the early problems which may arise when teaching beginners and some strategies to try. However, there are no hard-and-fast solutions to every problem, and teachers will have to develop a repertoire of strategies which they can then try out. If one strategy fails, teachers should try another.

Problem	Possible cause	Try
Shaking	Fear Cold	Encouragement Lots of fun and fast activities A heated pool
Eyes burning	Rubbing eyes Water chemical imbalance Prolonged water immersion	Beginner to blink the eyes Beginner to wear goggles
Will not open eyes under water	Fear	Beginner to wear goggles or face mask Fun activities using bright, colourful toys
Will not blow bubbles	Fear of putting face near water Cold	Encouragement Practise breathing skills Beginner to wear snorkel and mask
Holding onto the edge	Fear	Encouragement Beginner to use flotation aids
Feet glued to the bottom	Fear	Encouragement Beginner to use flotation aids Lots of fun games

First experience

In a relaxed situation, the teacher can observe students. For example, which students are timid and which are confident?

Scoop as much water as possible with toys, hands, buckets ...

Big circles   Little circles

Stir water with one foot, then the other.

Scoop water/ pour water.

If confident, try making rain.

Entering the water

Hold the edge, a flotation aid, or a partner's hand ...

Do a slide-in entry ...

Enter backwards on a ladder.

...for balance and confidence.

...at the side of the pool.

Confident beginners first, one step at a time, slowly!

Leaving the water

Aim: Safety for themselves and others

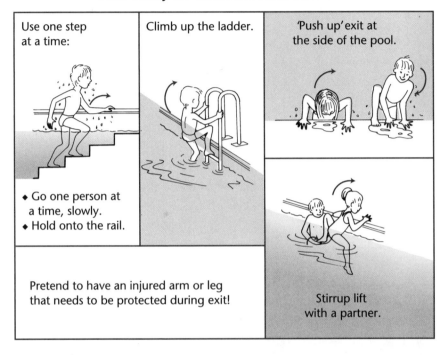

Use one step at a time:

- Go one person at a time, slowly.
- Hold onto the rail.

Pretend to have an injured arm or leg that needs to be protected during exit!

Climb up the ladder.

'Push up' exit at the side of the pool.

Stirrup lift with a partner.

Moving through the water

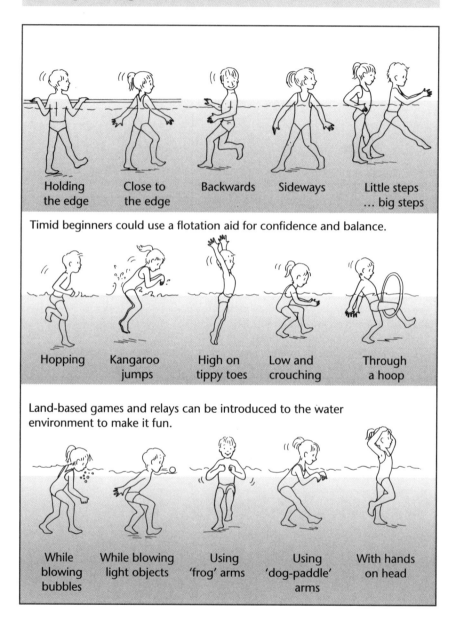

Holding the edge · Close to the edge · Backwards · Sideways · Little steps … big steps

Timid beginners could use a flotation aid for confidence and balance.

Hopping · Kangaroo jumps · High on tippy toes · Low and crouching · Through a hoop

Land-based games and relays can be introduced to the water environment to make it fun.

While blowing bubbles · While blowing light objects · Using 'frog' arms · Using 'dog-paddle' arms · With hands on head

Getting the face wet

Submerging

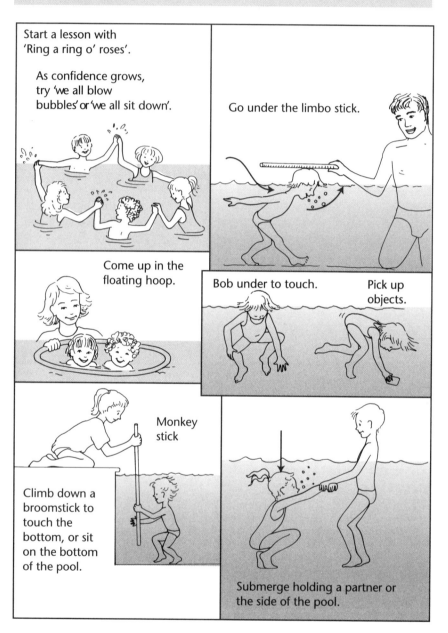

Start a lesson with 'Ring a ring o' roses'.

As confidence grows, try 'we all blow bubbles' or 'we all sit down'.

Go under the limbo stick.

Come up in the floating hoop.

Bob under to touch.

Pick up objects.

Monkey stick

Climb down a broomstick to touch the bottom, or sit on the bottom of the pool.

Submerge holding a partner or the side of the pool.

Opening eyes under water

Look at the hands and feet under water.

Count a partner's fingers.

Watch a partner's bubbles or make faces.

Pick up a certain color ring or object.

Act out different actions described on waterproof flashcards.

Regaining the standing position

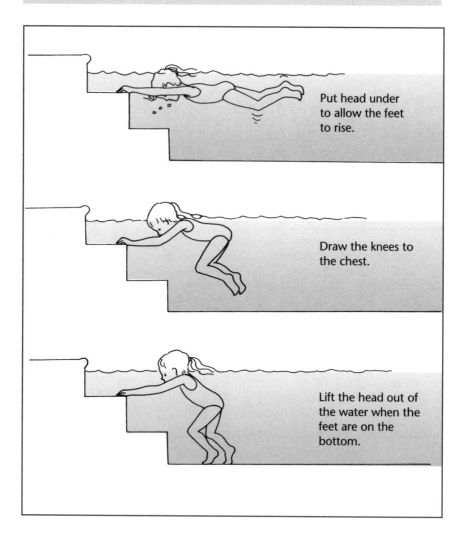

Put head under to allow the feet to rise.

Draw the knees to the chest.

Lift the head out of the water when the feet are on the bottom.

Regaining the standing position (continued)

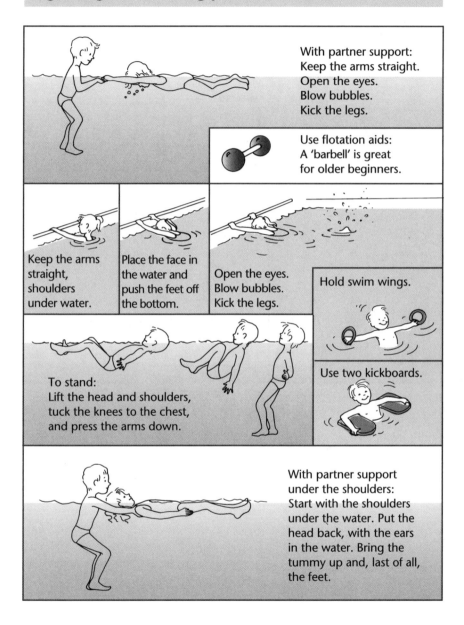

With partner support:
Keep the arms straight.
Open the eyes.
Blow bubbles.
Kick the legs.

Use flotation aids:
A 'barbell' is great
for older beginners.

Keep the arms straight, shoulders under water.

Place the face in the water and push the feet off the bottom.

Open the eyes.
Blow bubbles.
Kick the legs.

Hold swim wings.

To stand:
Lift the head and shoulders, tuck the knees to the chest, and press the arms down.

Use two kickboards.

With partner support under the shoulders:
Start with the shoulders under the water. Put the head back, with the ears in the water. Bring the tummy up and, last of all, the feet.

Breathing activities

Safety skills

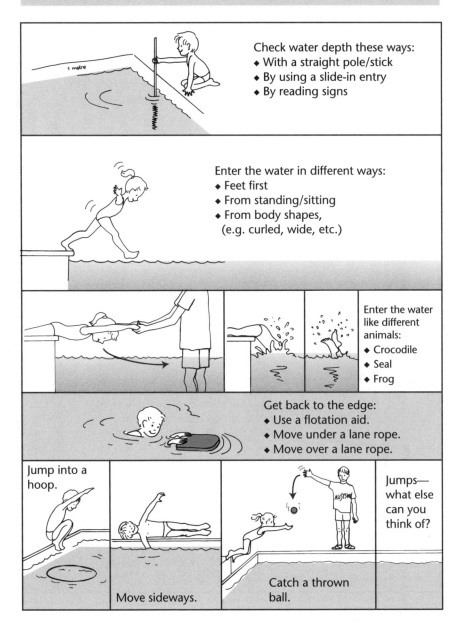

Check water depth these ways:
♦ With a straight pole/stick
♦ By using a slide-in entry
♦ By reading signs

Enter the water in different ways:
♦ Feet first
♦ From standing/sitting
♦ From body shapes,
  (e.g. curled, wide, etc.)

Enter the water like different animals:
♦ Crocodile
♦ Seal
♦ Frog

Get back to the edge:
♦ Use a flotation aid.
♦ Move under a lane rope.
♦ Move over a lane rope.

Jump into a hoop.

Move sideways.

Catch a thrown ball.

Jumps—what else can you think of?

Basic rescue skills

Aim: To teach the beginner how to rescue without entering the water, and how it feels to be rescued

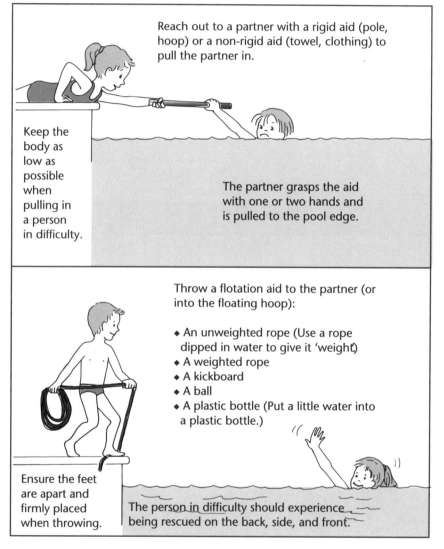

Reach out to a partner with a rigid aid (pole, hoop) or a non-rigid aid (towel, clothing) to pull the partner in.

Keep the body as low as possible when pulling in a person in difficulty.

The partner grasps the aid with one or two hands and is pulled to the pool edge.

Throw a flotation aid to the partner (or into the floating hoop):

- An unweighted rope (Use a rope dipped in water to give it 'weight')
- A weighted rope
- A kickboard
- A ball
- A plastic bottle (Put a little water into a plastic bottle.)

Ensure the feet are apart and firmly placed when throwing.

The person in difficulty should experience being rescued on the back, side, and front.

Chapter 3

FLOATING AND MOVEMENT SKILLS

Buoyancy

The aims of this stage are for beginners to become confident in their ability to float independently in different positions and be able to return to a standing position. Many people have difficulty in achieving a motionless float because of the high proportion of muscle and bone in the body, and they may have to use sculling actions to maintain surface buoyancy. In these cases it will be necessary to combine buoyancy and mobility activities.

Students at this level need to learn to raise their feet off the bottom of the pool, become fully supported by the water and then return to the standing position. To accomplish this, they need activities that will help them to discover and understand the buoyancy characteristics of water. The major objectives of this stage are an understanding of flotation principles, the development of flotation skills and the ability to return to a standing position. The following experiences should be included:

- Floating on the front, back and side on the surface of the water
- Using the limbs to maintain a horizontal float
- Using the limbs to maintain a vertical float
- Using the limbs to maintain an underwater position
- Breathing activities
- Water safety activities using flotation aids

During the teaching of the buoyancy stage, teachers may need to call on skills from the water familiarisation and mobility stages to help beginners relax and grow in confidence.

Lesson plans during the teaching of the buoyancy stage should include the following:

- New, enjoyable activities to introduce mobility to beginners
- Activities that reinforce water familiarisation skills
- Buoyancy skills practice

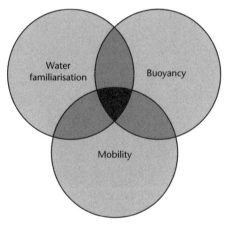

The total swimming program.

Floating on the Front

Teachers can introduce floating in shallow water with beginners holding onto the side or edge with their feet on the bottom. The torso is extended and the chin is on the surface. A full breath is taken, and the face is placed in the water and held there while the teacher counts slowly to three. To exaggerate the effect of buoyancy, beginners should exhale slowly while under the water and thus feel their bodies sink farther as more weight is placed on their feet.

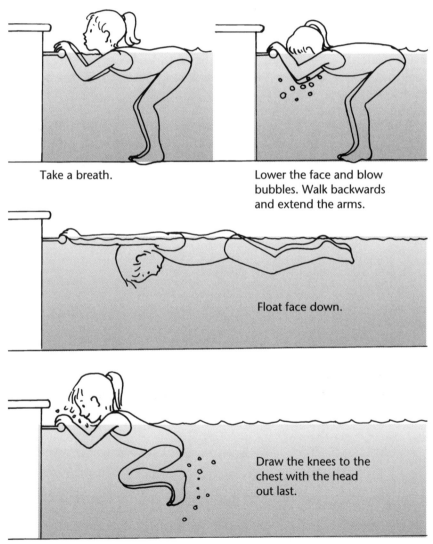

Take a breath.

Lower the face and blow bubbles. Walk backwards and extend the arms.

Float face down.

Draw the knees to the chest with the head out last.

Learning to float face downwards.

The head should then be raised slowly to just clear the mouth from the water and the previous action repeated. The teacher could ask beginners what is holding the body up or whether they are able to feel the rise and fall of the body, then ask about the reason for this.

From the same starting position, beginners can take a deep breath, hold it fully, extend the body and try to wash the back of the head or look for the navel while placing the face in the water.

Many beginners will find that the feet naturally float to the surface and that the body will not sink. Others may need to be encouraged or even directed to allow the feet to float upwards.

When first teaching students to return to a standing position from a floating position, directions should be given regarding tucking of both knees and lifting the head to assist with the action. Many beginners need to practise with assistance to avoid a loss of confidence.

When beginners have achieved reasonable success in floating with their faces in the water (but with both hands still holding the wall), a further stage could be to repeat the activity, but when the feet have floated up to the surface, allow one hand to gently let go of the wall and float free.

Progressions

- One hand grasps the wrist of the hand holding the wall. This hand is released when the feet float.

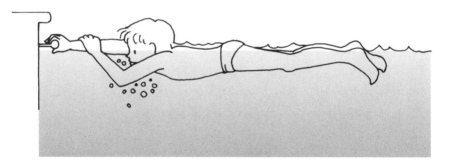

- The above is repeated but with both hands letting go of the wall and pressing down in the standing-up stage. (Sometimes beginners are more confident working with a partner for this exercise.)

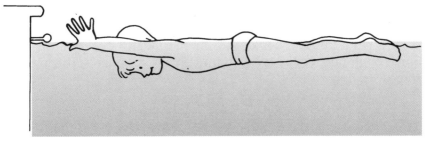

- One person stands in front of another who assumes the floating position. The supporting partner does not let the floating partner drift away.

- The person takes a small step away from the wall and reaches forwards to float into the wall, but remains in a float position, holding the wall for a count of three. This can be repeated, the person progressively moving farther from the wall.

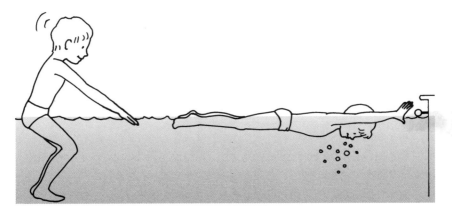

Encourage beginners to open their eyes (looking for objects, fish or the wall). For those who are less confident, the teacher may place a hand under the water for them to watch or reach towards. Some beginners could try a swim belt for confidence during this stage.

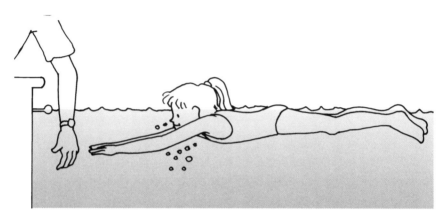

Standing up before reaching the wall should then be introduced. Then, facing away from the wall, beginners can float or glide like a long, narrow arrow away from the pool edge, to see how far they can go.

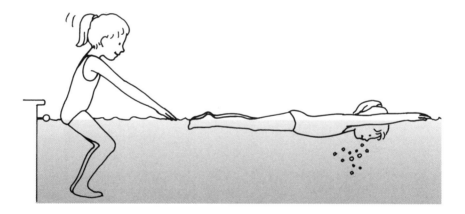

This all can be practised using flotation aids and/or a partner for support.

Practices in Shallow Open Water

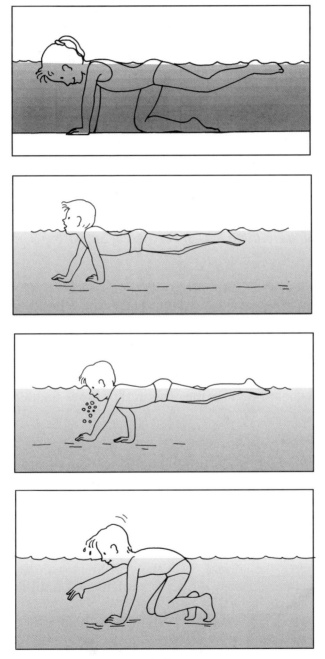

Learning to float face downwards in shallow water.

- From a kneeling position, with the hands apart on the bottom of the pool or river, beginners place the face in the water, straighten one leg at a time and allow it to float up to the surface.
- With the chin in the water, beginners take a full breath, place the face down in the water and allow the legs to float up to a relaxed (wide) position. They then ease air slowly out of the nose. With the chin alternately in the water and on the surface, they walk the hands along the bottom like a crocodile, expelling the air noisily.
- Beginners place the face in the water with both hands on the bottom and, as the feet float up, allow one hand to float up gently. They then stand by pressing down with the floating hand, pulling the knees up and raising the head.

When teaching beginners to float, partners and/or flotation aids are useful if there are no walls to hold.

Activities Using Flotation Aids or Partner for Support

Beginners

- adopt the elbow support position on a kickboard, place the face in the water, extend the legs slowly backwards and exhale air slowly through the nose.
- repeat the above actions, using the fingers-on-top-thumbs-underneath grip of the kickboard. Upon reaching the front float position, they drum the fingers or 'play the piano' on the kickboard to relax the arms and improve floating.

Floating on the Back

Floating on the back can be learned initially in very shallow water. Beginners sit in the pool with the hands resting behind the hips and lean backwards until the elbows rest on the bottom. From the elbow rest position, the upper body leans back until the shoulders and back of the head submerge and the top of the forehead is level with the surface of the water. From this position, the hips are pushed towards the surface, with the eyes looking up at the sky. This is repeated and then the arms straightened until fingertips provide the only support.

An alternative is to sit on the bottom and hold a buoyant aid such as a kickboard or large ball close to the chest. Beginners slowly lean back, lower the back of the head into the water, extend the hips and look up.

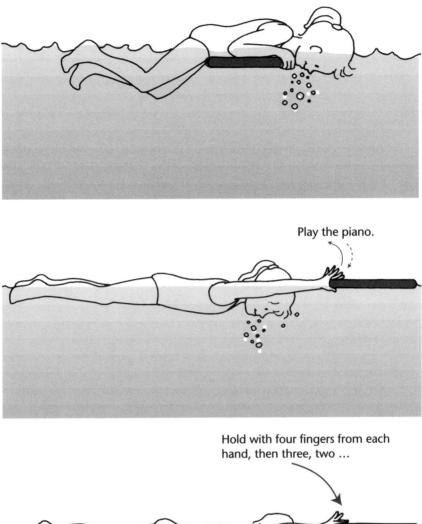

Play the piano.

Hold with four fingers from each hand, then three, two …

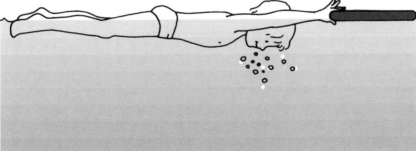

Floating practice using a kickboard.

Mushroom float.   Floating face downwards.

If shallow water is unavailable, another way of learning a back float is with a partner providing support under the shoulders. Beginners bend the knees until the shoulders are under the water.

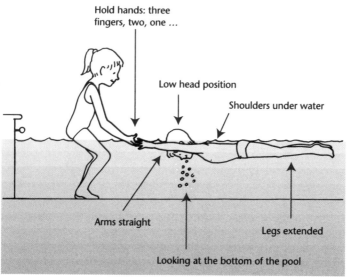

Floating with partner support.

The head is back and the hips extend until the body is horizontal and the head and chest clear of the water.

Learning to float on the back in shallow water.

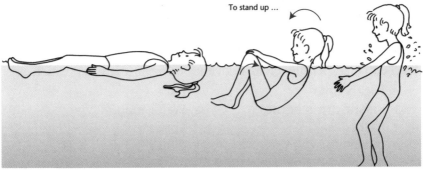
To stand up ...

Regaining balance from floating on the back.

Experiment with floating on the back using this equipment:

- Kickboards
- Swim wings
- Swim belts
- Buckets
- Balls

Try variations on back floats:

- Using different letters
- Using different shapes

To stand up, beginners tuck the chin into the chest, pull the knees upwards as the hips sink and extend the legs to stand.

Floating on the Side

Many of the shallow water activities mentioned in the front and back float sections can be used to teach the side float:

- Using the elbow for support
- With kickboard held over the hips

Drawing the legs towards the chest will cause the body to rotate onto the front. The remaining movements are the same as for the front float recovery.

Using the Limbs to Maintain an Underwater Position

Beginners should be provided with an opportunity to explore the various limb actions required to maintain an underwater position. The following activities should only be carried out in clear water:

- In shallow water, lying on the back or front on the bottom of the pool
- In waist- or chest-deep water:
  - various body positions (front, back, curled, wide, etc.)
  - various depths (midway, bottom, surface)

Students can perform these activities while blowing big bubbles, slow bubbles or no bubbles.

Experimenting With Buoyancy

Teachers can experiment with buoyancy using a variety of flotation aids:

- Kickboards
- Plastic drink bottles
- Ice boxes
- Buckets

- Balls
- Water mats
- Tubes
- Other flotation aids

The following activities will enable beginners to discover that various flotation aids have different degrees of buoyancy:

- Floating in different positions using various flotation aids
- Floating with an aid and then kicking to the edge
- Group floating
- Floating in different positions wearing a PFD
- Floating with a partner while sharing a PFD

Floating practice with aids.

Changing From One Flotation Position to Another

Beginners should change from one position to another. During the following floats, they should be encouraged to move slowly, keep the limbs in the water, feel for positions which are easiest to hold and move the limbs to maintain a balanced, buoyant position:

- Mushroom float
- Jellyfish float
- Star float (front/back)
- Turtle float (This is like a mushroom float, but the head is lifted to get another breath of air without standing. The head is then placed back in the water.)
- Different letters or shapes

Beginners can do these floats in various combinations (e.g. a star float on front, changing to a mushroom and twisting over to a back float).

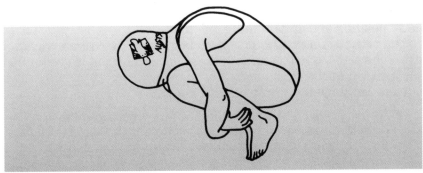

Mushroom float.

Breathing Activities

Breathing activities should constantly be reinforced with all practices:

- With support
- Without support
- Across the pool or over a distance

Water Safety Activities Using Flotation Aids

'Reach to rescue' skills, introduced in games and fun activities in the water familiarisation stage, can now be expanded to include the use of flotation aids and beginners' buoyancy skills.

Beginners

- assume different body positions and are towed in by a partner.
- use a flotation aid to float in various positions, then, on a signal, kick to the edge and climb out.
- enter the water while holding a flotation aid, float and then return to the edge.

- throw a flotation aid to a partner, instruct him or her to float on the back or front and then kick to the edge.
- enter the water wearing a PFD.
- climb onto an inflated raft or water mat and then paddle to the edge.

Movement Through the Water (Propulsion)

The aims of this section are to enable teachers to give beginners the opportunity to discover and explore limb movements that will propel them through the water in different body directions (head first, feet first and sideways) and to help beginners understand the principles of propulsion through the water, especially the effects of body position and streamlining.

The activities used should allow beginners to explore ways of using the arms, the legs or both the arms and legs to move on the surface or under water.

Here are some terms you should know:

- *A paired action.* A paired action occurs when both the arms or both the legs perform a similar action at the same time (e.g. the breaststroke arm action and the butterfly leg kick).
- *An underwater recovery.* An underwater recovery occurs when the arms are returned to a position under the water to begin the pull phase of the stroke (e.g. in the breaststroke and life-saving backstroke arm actions).
- *An alternate action.* An alternate action occurs when the propulsion phase of a stroke is being performed by one arm and/or leg while the other arm or leg is performing the recovery phase.
- *An above-water recovery.* An above-water recovery occurs when the arm is lifted out of the water as it returns to the entry position (e.g. in the front crawl arm action).
- *An independent action.* An independent action is one in which each limb follows a different movement pathway (e.g. the sidestroke arm and leg actions).

Gliding

Gliding skills should be consolidated before adding propulsion using the limbs. This can be achieved by holding a flotation aid in front with the arms extended. Beginners push off from the bottom, side or steps of the pool. They should be encouraged to open the eyes, blow bubbles and let the legs float freely behind.

Teachers should get beginners to try gliding variations such as these:

- With legs wide or together
- With legs curled
- Without a flotation aid
- Under water

Beginners can compare the distance travelled and discover the most effective technique. This helps to develop an understanding of streamlining.

Propulsion Using the Arms and Hands

Using the arms only, beginners should explore different ways to move through the water head first, feet first and sideways both on the water's surface and underwater.

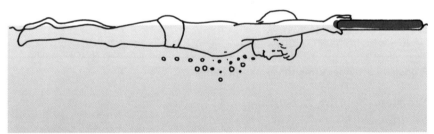

Push and glide on the front.

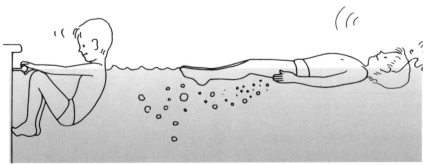

Push and glide on the back.

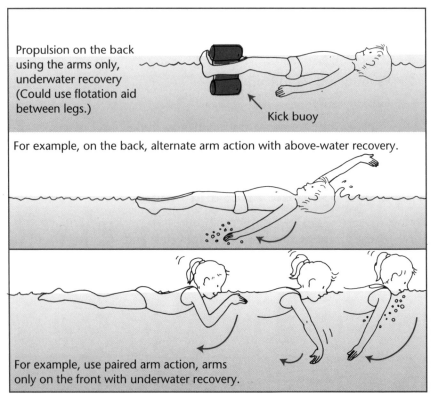

Propulsion on the back using the arms only, underwater recovery (Could use flotation aid between legs.)

Kick buoy

For example, on the back, alternate arm action with above-water recovery.

For example, use paired arm action, arms only on the front with underwater recovery.

Propelling activities using the arms and hands.

Problem-Solving Activities
Beginners

- use an alternate arm action to move head first through the water with both above-water and underwater arm recoveries.
- use a paired arm action to move head first through the water with both above-water and underwater arm recoveries.
- keep the arms near the side and find various ways of using the arms and hands to move head first and feet first. This activity can be tried with the arms held out beyond the head or underneath the body.

Beginners can try these activities on the back and the side.

Teachers should encourage beginners to invent their own ways of moving through the water using alternate, independent and paired leg and arm actions with both above-water and underwater recoveries.

Propulsion Using the Legs and Feet

Setting the task of using the legs and feet for propulsion, beginners move through the water head first, both on the water's surface and underwater.

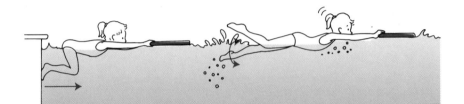

Propulsion using the legs and feet.

Problem-Solving Activities
The following activities can be done with or without a flotation aid. Beginners

- push off from the wall, steps or bottom of the pool and move the legs.
- perform a different alternate, independent or paired leg action each time.
- try the previous activities on the back and side.
- stop and compare the action, asking questions such as these:
  - 'What action made the most splash?'
  - 'What action was the easiest?'
  - 'What action pushed you the longest distance?'

The Torpedo

The torpedo is a combination of a glide with an alternate (flutter) kick. Teachers should encourage beginners to use a relaxed leg action originating from the hips, with the legs long and loose (like kicking off your socks without the use of your hands). Beginners should try the following:

- The torpedo on the back and side
- The torpedo with flippers

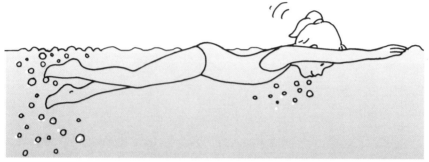

The torpedo.

Propulsion Forwards, Backwards and Sideways

Leg and arm actions are now combined to explore different ways of moving forwards, backwards or sideways on the surface and under water.

Problem-Solving Activities
Beginners

- use combinations of paired arm and leg actions, with various recoveries and in various body positions.
- use combinations of alternate arm and leg actions with various recoveries and in various body positions.
- use different leg and arm actions to move head first, feet first or sideways in a circle.
- use alternate arm and leg actions to move head first, do four alternate arm actions on the front (face down), then roll onto the back and repeat (breathing while on the back, blowing bubbles while on the front).
- try the previous actions using paired arm and leg actions.
- propel themselves through submerged hoops or through their partners' legs.
- submerge and use the legs and arms to return to the surface feet first, head first or sideways.
- return to the surface vertically or sideways head first and assume different body shapes from an underwater position.

Breathing Activities

During the water familiarisation stage, breathing activities were introduced. Now that beginners are more confident in their mobility skills, more advanced breathing activities can be introduced.

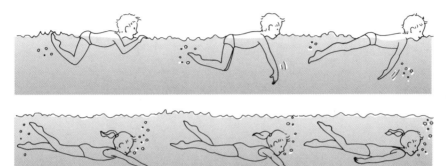

Problem-solving activities to develop propulsive technique.

Problem-Solving Activities
Beginners

- walk and inhale, then submerge and exhale (every three steps).

Breathing practice and walking.

- while standing, turn the head to one side (one ear in the water) and inhale, then roll the face into the water and exhale.

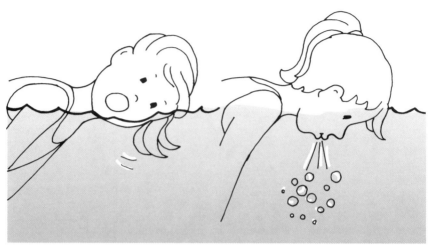

Breathing practice while rotating the head to the side.

- walk with hands behind the back and the face in the water, turn so one ear is in the water, inhale, then, on rolling the face back into the water, exhale.

Breathing practice while walking and turning the head to the side.

- try the previous activities while doing different arm actions (e.g. paired and alternate).

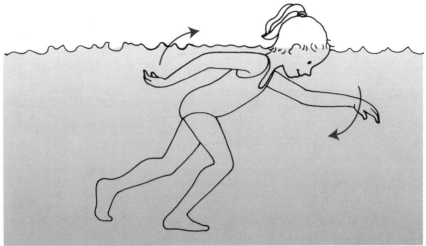

Breathing practice with different arm actions.

- using a flotation aid for support, kick across the pool, completing the breathing actions on the right side, then the left side.
- using different arm and leg actions, try breathing to the front (as in the breaststroke).

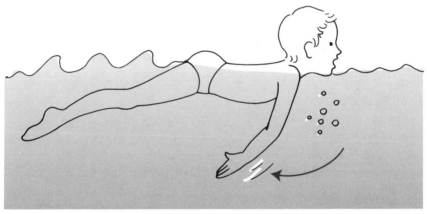

Breathing action with different limb movements.

For beginners who are too busy concentrating on the arm action and breathing to remember to kick the legs, a flotation aid such as a swim belt may be useful.

Distances should gradually be increased and a rhythmical breathing action encouraged.

Sculling

Sculling is the basic skill upon which all strokes and many other techniques are based. Sculling movements resemble the action of a ship's screw propeller and involve changing the pitch of the hands for the most effective propulsion through the water or for the maintenance of a stable body position.

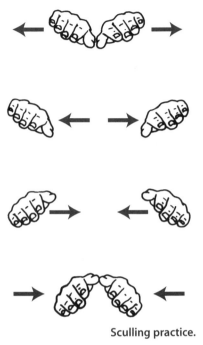

Sculling Practice

On the Edge of the Pool or Flat Surface

During the outward sweep the hands are angled, palms outwards at approximately 45°. With the little fingers leading, beginners run the thumbs along the surface. They stop the outward sweep and rotate the hands (palms inwards) when the elbows are almost straight.

Sculling practice.

During the inward sweep, the hands are angled, palms inwards at approximately 45°. With the thumbs leading, beginners run the little fingers along the surface back together.

Standing in Shallow Water

Standing in shallow water, beginners should practise the outward and inward sweep of the sculling action, keeping the upper arms reasonably still and allowing the hands and forearms to move outwards and inwards in relaxed, smooth but firm, continuous movements.

Standing in Shoulder-Deep Water

Standing in shoulder-deep water and sculling, beginners bend both knees and lift the feet gently off the bottom of the pool. It is important for teachers to encourage the application of equal pressure against the water on both the outward and inward sweeps. The lifting effect of the scull can be improved by increasing the speed of the action.

Sculling practice in shoulder-deep water.

Checklist

- Hands are flat (not cupped).
- Hands are angled at 45°.
- Hands move horizontally.
- Upper arms are relatively still.
- Action is relaxed, smooth, firm and continuous.

Stationary Sculling (Flat Sculling)

Stationary sculling is used to maintain a stationary position and to gain lift. This is achieved by holding the fingertips at the same level as the wrist.

Stationary sculling.

Head-First Sculling

The arms are held by the sides and a streamlined back float position is adopted. The hand position is with the fingertips tilted up towards the surface of the water.

◄————— Direction of travel

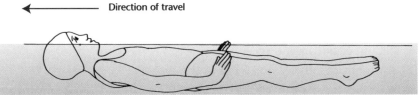

Head-first sculling.

Feet-First Sculling

For feet-first sculling the below position is adopted and the fingertips are tilted down towards the bottom of the pool.

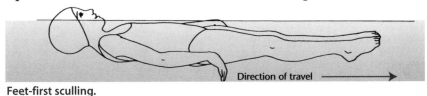

Direction of travel ————►

Feet-first sculling.

Further Practice

In chest-deep water, beginners could use a sculling action and lift their feet off the bottom. In a back float and then front float position, with their arms by their sides, they perform

- a stationary scull,
- a head-first scull, and
- a feet-first scull.

Beginners can practise sculling while in a tucked position, using the hands alternately to rotate the body.

Water Safety Activities

Water safety activities at this stage should reinforce beginners' skills in combining the use of buoyancy aids with the alternative methods of propulsion to assist in performing a self-rescue. Beginners

- are towed in by a rope rescue, assisting the rescuer by kicking the legs.
- try the previous rope rescue using different body positions.
- using the arms, legs, or arms and legs, move to a floating buoyant rescue aid.
- submerge and surface next to a buoyancy aid.
- pretend that they have been injured and, using aids thrown to them, propel themselves to the edge of the pool.
- pretend that they are in deep water, float on the back and then kick to the edge.
- practise putting on a PFD in the water.
- while wearing a PFD, try various arm and leg swimming actions.

Introduction to Deep Water

Eventually, the time comes when teachers must decide whether their beginners are ready to be introduced to deep water. Water is considered deep when beginners cannot stand on the bottom with the mouth clear of the surface.

Some beginners are enthusiastic; others may be apprehensive about the thought of the deep end even though they feel confident in the water.

Some teachers believe in introducing deep water activities very early in the program. Others want the beginners to be able to float. Others again require that beginners be able to 'swim' certain distances before they allow them near deep water. The time is right when teachers decide the moment has come for their particular class! Teachers should know the individual characteristics of the students and what their students can cope with. However, safety, encouragement and patience are the key words for deep water experience activities.

It is important that beginners be aware that when they submerge vertically into water, care should be taken to avoid water being forced up the nostrils. The blowing of 'nose bubbles' should be encouraged at all times.

Deep Water Activities

Beginners

- walk hand over hand along the wall (crab crawling) from the shallow end to the deep end.
- submerge slowly, while holding the edge with the hands, until the arms are fully extended.
- bob up and down while holding the edge and blowing nose bubbles.
- face the edge and relax, letting legs hang. They then take a breath and put the face into the water (to look at the feet).
- submerge while holding onto the edge with one hand only.
- form into pairs, facing one another. Each person holds onto the side of the pool with one hand and their partner's hand with the other. They then both float face down.
- form into pairs, one floating face down, first letting go of the edge and then of the partner's hand. The partner still holds out the hand for the 'floater' to grab if necessary.
- facing the edge with chins in the water, take a breath and then let go of the edge and let their bodies sink (vertical float).
- try the vertical float with arms above the head.
- submerge (while close to the wall), touch the bottom and push off to resurface. This activity should be started in water that is not too deep.

- play 'Fireman's Pole'—climbing down the pole feet first until the feet touch the bottom and, as confidence grows, climbing down and picking up an object.
- jump in and hold onto a hoop (strong) or a puppet rope held by the teacher.
- jump in, surface and grasp the pole held by the teacher. (It may be held 1 to 2 metres (3 to 6 feet) away if the teacher knows that students will move towards it.)
- jump in and move unassisted to the side, with the pole held nearby should it be needed.
- slide in, attached to a puppet rope held by the teacher and kick on the back along the side of the wall.
- float using a flotation aid (e.g. a PFD).

Treading Water

Treading water can be very tiring for beginners, and teachers should take all safety precautions into consideration when teaching this skill.

Beginners practise treading water in these ways:

- Holding onto the edge with one hand
- Using swim wings, a swim belt or another device
- Holding a flotation aid
- Using a PFD
- Using a puppet rope held by the teacher
- When close to the edge of the pool
- With horizontal arm sculling
- Using different leg actions (e.g. flutter kick, breaststroke kick, scissors kick)

Entries and Exits

The how, why and when of entries into the water should be discussed with beginners:

- How to perform the entries with safety
- Why certain entries are used (e.g. a 'step in' entry is used when the water is clear, the depth is known, and the bottom is clear of obstacles)
- When to use certain entries (e.g. diving into deep water)

Activities

Beginners

- jump into the water from various heights (e.g. pool edge, starting blocks, diving boards).
- jump into the water wearing a PFD.
- slide in, pretend there is an obstacle and climb back out.
- do a kneeling dive, float or tread water, then swim unassisted to the edge and climb out.
- catch a flotation aid thrown by the teacher and use it to kick back to the edge and climb out.

Games

Games make the learning of swimming an enjoyable experience and help beginners learn water skills through play. Following are some of the games and activities which teachers may use. Additional games are included in specialised publications such as *Wet Games* by P. Meaney and S. Culka (Robert Anderson, Clifton Hill, Vic., 1992). Many other land-based games and activities can be adapted for the water. When considering conducting games in the water, teachers should consider the age and the ability of each group member, the number of participants, water space and conditions and the availability of equipment.

Ring a Ring o'Roses

Number
Four or more

Organisation
In a circle with hands joined

Area
Shallow water

Equipment
None

Description

In waist-deep water, the class joins hands in a circle. Walking in a clockwise direction, they sing:

Ring a ring o' roses
A pocket full o' posies
Ah'tishoo, ah'tishoo
We all fall down.

As 'down' is sung, all the students submerge.

Variations

We all blow bubbles.
We all sit down.

Follow the Leader

Number
Four or more

Organisation
Students line up behind the leader

Area
Shallow water

Equipment
None or hoops, dive ring, etc.

Description
In waist-deep water, students line up behind the leader, who takes them through a number of movements that the teacher asks of them (e.g. walking, running, moving forwards and backwards, zigzagging, hopping, picking up a ring, moving through a hoop). Change leaders often so all students get a chance to lead.

Chain Reaction

Number
Four or more

Organisation
In a circle

Area
Shallow water

Equipment
None

Description
In waist-deep water, the group stands in a circle. The teacher chooses the starter, who must then perform an action (e.g. blow bubbles) that each student in turn must copy. The next turn goes to the student on the right of the starter. It is then his or her turn to choose an activity and add it to the previous one.

Flashcards

Number
Four or more

Organisation
In a line facing the teacher

Area
Shallow water

Equipment
Flashcards such as $(2 + ... = 4)$ or $(5 - ... = 3)$

Description
Students must collect rings or table tennis balls from the surface or bottom that would total the numbers missing from the cards.

Splish Splash

Number
Six or more

Organisation
In two teams

Area
Shallow water

Equipment
One large plastic jug and one kickboard per team

Description
In waist-deep water each team forms a circle. A plastic jug with no lid is placed in the centre on a kickboard. On the signal 'Go', all students begin splashing water into their team's jug. No student may touch the jug. The team to fill the jug first is the winner.

Simon Says

Number
Four or more

Organisation
Individual

Area
Shallow water

Description
Play the game of 'Simon Says' with activities designed to give confidence in the water. If the teacher prefaces a command with 'Simon Says', all students must obey. Anyone who does not is out of the game. If the teacher does not preface a command with 'Simon Says', anyone who does obey the command is out of the game. The last person left is the winner and becomes the new 'Simon'.

Chapter 4

APPLICATION OF PRINCIPLES OF MOVEMENT IN WATER

The actions of swimmers in water are dependent upon natural forces and their interaction with various internal forces generated by the swimmer. By understanding these forces and relationships and how they influence the body in water, swimming teachers can utilise the positive aspects and maximise facilitation of skill learning.

Biomechanics is considered to be the physics of how the body moves. Biomechanics involves an integrated study between the internal forces produced by the body and the naturally occurring external forces that act on the body as skills are executed.

An understanding of biomechanics assists in

- improving performance,
- preventing injury,
- correcting weaknesses, and
- identifying ways to alter human movement patterns.

Of particular interest to swimming teachers is the investigation of how the human body and the forces it generates maximise the naturally occurring forces of water.

As swimmers more fully comprehend the forces acting on them and around them, they will become more proficient at using them to their advantage. The more efficient the swimmer, the better use he or she makes of the environment.

Buoyancy/Flotation

Every object that is immersed in water is subject to an upward force action through the centre of buoyancy and a downward force action through the centre of gravity. These two opposing forces, acting through different locations in the body, produce rotating forces that result in a small body rotation. Generally, the swimmer's legs will sink lower than the upper body, as they are denser than the water they have displaced. The position at which the body will come to rest and float in the water is found when the centre of the body's weight (center of gravity) aligns itself vertically with the centre of the water displaced (center of buoyancy).

It should be noted that even if a body floats in a horizontal position, both the centre of buoyancy and the centre of gravity may still be vertically aligned. This situation can occur in young children and some adult females, but very few adult males!

The position in which a body will float in water is the result of the counter forces of the centre of buoyancy and the centre of gravity, while the ability of a body to float is determined by the density of the body relative to the density of the water. A person who is able to float with ease is likely to learn to swim more readily than one who has difficulty in floating. Any movement or rotation that occurs during floating will therefore be the result of the centre of gravity and the centre of buoyancy being out of alignment. Factors that may cause this to occur include shape and symmetry.

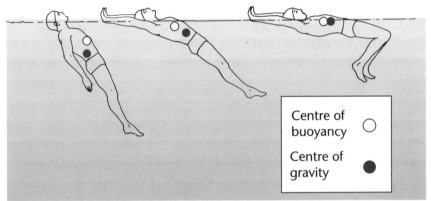

Centre of buoyancy ○

Centre of gravity ●

Centre of gravity and centre of buoyancy in vertical alignment.

Shape

The position of the limbs and head can drastically alter the floating position of the body. Changes in the shape of the body that shift weight towards the head result in the centre of gravity shifting in the same direction. This assists the body to achieve a horizontal, motionless floating position as the centre of buoyancy and the centre of gravity become aligned.

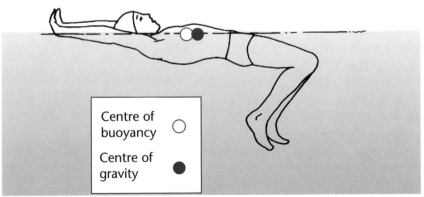

Centre of buoyancy ○

Centre of gravity ●

Floating horizontally with the centre of gravity and the centre of buoyancy in vertical alignment.

Swimmers should be encouraged to experiment with different body shapes on their backs, fronts and sides to gain an appreciation of how different body shapes will affect floating. A novel way to enable beginners to learn new shapes is to get them to form as many letters as possible (e.g. X, Y, I, T, O, L, A).

Symmetry and Asymmetry

Symmetry is another factor which affects the way in which the body floats. A symmetrical, evenly proportioned body which is regular in form may float in a balanced plane. An asymmetric body will not be evenly proportioned and is unlikely to float in an even plane.

Most human bodies have some form of asymmetry. For example, a good tennis player will have greater muscular development in one arm than the other; an older adult with a hip replacement will be asymmetric. In both cases, the position of the centre of gravity will be affected and will necessitate a change in body shape to maintain a position of balance in water.

Rotation

Rotation occurs when the centre of gravity and the centre of buoyancy are not in alignment. Rotation can be destabilising during floating but can be controlled and used for recovering from a float.

Vertical rotation is movement forwards or backwards about a central pivot. This direction of rotation is required when recovering from a front or back floating position to standing.

Lateral rotation occurs from side to side around the long axis of the body. The body rotates quickly around this axis due to very little resistance from the water. This rotation can be controlled by changing the body shape.

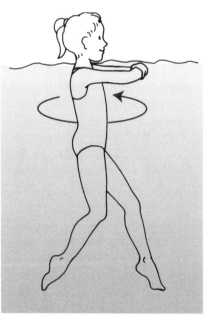

Lateral rotation in the vertical plane.

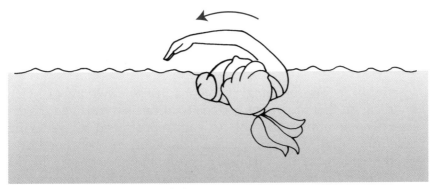

Lateral rotation in the horizontal plane.

Applying Principles of Movement in Water to Strokes

Efficient technique for survival and competitive swimming strokes is dependent on the application of the principles of resistance and propulsion. While each stroke has individual characteristics, teachers must understand both the positive and negative aspects of these principles to enhance the development of swimmers' techniques and allow them to gain maximum performance from a minimal energy output.

Following are four common faults which may confront the novice teacher:

- **Sinking.** In a stationary position, the body will sink if the swimmer does not have the capacity to float (e.g. has little body fat and is unable to stabilise in the floating position). However, if the swimmer sinks while performing a stroke or drill, she or he is failing to produce the right amount of lift force to keep her or him afloat. This is usually the result of poor sculling technique and an inefficient kick, which causes the body to lose balance. Good underwater arm and hand actions will ensure sinking does not happen.

- **Moving backwards.** When beginners try to perform a drill or complete stroke, sometimes they do not travel efficiently and appear to stay in the same place or even move backwards. This is a reflection of the body's inability to catch water, grip onto it and travel forward by extending the arm.

Excessive turbulence is often created by the dragging of air bubbles under water. When eddies form around the body, suction prevents forward movement. A good streamlined position plus effective arm and leg actions will prevent backward movement. Isolated drill work will overcome many major stroke problems.

- **Bobbing**. The 'bobbing' action of a freestyle swimmer is often an indication that the upper body is rotating as the arm enters the water. The swimmer attempts to gain more speed by achieving maximum distance per arm stroke. This effort can be ruined by a bobbing action, as the swimmer spears the arm deeply in the water. Often the shoulder of the entering arm will submerge and create excessive movement on the long axis.

The head may also move, which will cause a body imbalance. The head should be fixed in freestyle because it acts as the control point. A smooth, rhythmical arm action and a still head are encouraged if a swimmer experiences bobbing. Bobbing is common in overenthusiastic swimmers who are striving to force their strokes into a faster rhythm.

- **Zigzagging**. Beginner swimmers often travel from side to side in a zigzag pattern. Any sideways movement is a result of the body trying to balance itself. Remember the theorem 'for every action there is an equal and opposite reaction'. In freestyle, when the arm enters the water across the body, the legs will try to balance the body and so a zigzag or 'snaking' action will occur.

For each alternate arm entry, the legs move wide (outside the streamlined position of the body) and cause a zigzag. The swimmer can overcome this problem by using an efficient arm entry and catch and a strong, effective flutter kick and by learning to be long and streamlined without going outside the correct arm and leg movement areas.

Novice teachers may consider the following to assist with the application of the principles of resistance and propulsion:

- The position of the head largely determines the position of the body in the water.
- It is important to ensure that beginners acquire a streamlined body position during elementary stroke learning drills and maintain the streamlined position throughout stroke performance.

- Both the hands/arms and the legs/feet propel the body through the water, with the former usually producing the most force.
- The legs and feet assist with stabilising the body and keep it streamlined.
- The back of the hand usually faces the direction of preferred travel.

The freestyle stroke provides a good example of how principles of movement may be applied to strokes.

Freestyle

Resistance

The position of the body during freestyle should be as horizontal as possible—at or just below the surface of the water, depending on the body composition of the swimmer. During elementary push and glide drills the depth of the head in the water should be adjusted to enable the heels of the feet to be at the surface of the water. Lifting the head will increase drag by 20 to 35 per cent.

The overall streamlined position enables frontal resistance to be minimised. The streamlining also serves to reduce eddy resistance. Frictional resistance cannot be effectively reduced and is therefore not considered.

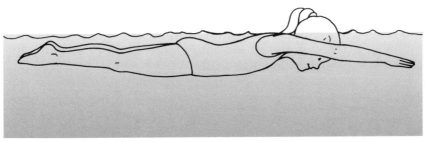

Streamlined body position.

The body, as viewed from above, should remain in a straight line. The rolling or swaying effect from the arm action should be minimised by ensuring that each hand does not cross the midline of the body and refraining from swinging arms wide to the side.

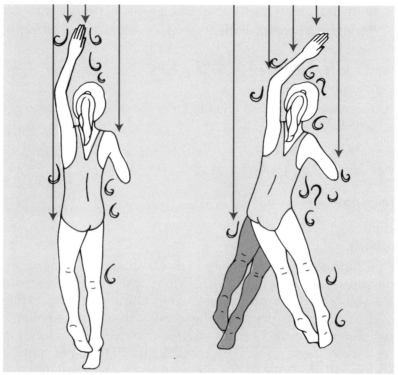

The effect of excessive side-to-side body movements.

Propulsion

The arms and hands provide the major propulsion in freestyle. Key considerations for efficient propulsion include the following:

1. The hand enters the water with minimal resistance—'spearing the water'. It is usual for the thumb and index finger to enter first, followed by the wrist, forearm and elbow. During the entry the elbow is kept higher than the wrist.

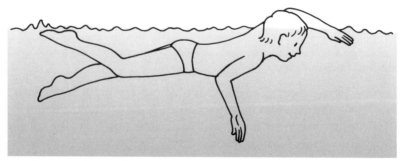

Hand entry position in freestyle.

2. Following the entry the hand slides forwards and downwards until the arm straightens and the little finger begins to sweep outwards and downwards in a curvilinear path to 'catch' the water. The elbow gradually flexes to allow the palm of the hand to face backwards. The hand is now in a position to apply a force against the water and so propel the body forwards. This action is related to the principle of 'propulsive drag'.

3. The insweep is the first propulsive phase of an arm stroke. The hand moves in a semicircular motion to allow the hand and forearm to press firmly against still water. If the water begins to move backwards, the application of force is significantly reduced.

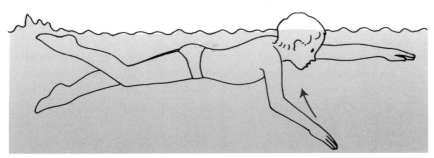

Position of arm during insweep.

4. The upsweep is the second and final phase of the arm stroke. It commences at the completion of the insweep and continues until the hand reaches the thigh. The elbow extends during the upsweep. During the insweep and upsweep the hand accelerates and the hand pitches to push backwards against the water.

5. At the conclusion of the propulsive phase it is important that the hand leave the water at the point where the hand releases pressure on the water to minimise resistance.

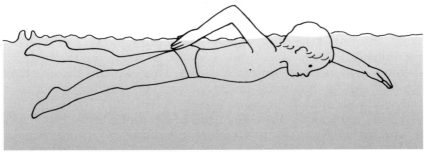

Hand leaving the water with minimal splash.

Propulsion—Legs and Feet

The legs and feet provide a stabilising force with a minor but important role in aiding propulsion. Of particular importance, however, is the impact the kicking action has on assisting the body in an almost horizontal and streamlined position. A flutter kick exceeding a depth of 30 centimetres (12 inches) causes frontal resistance, thus reducing speed. A deep kick may also affect the body position and cause eddies to form at the back of the legs.

To provide drive and propulsion from the kick, the toes must be pointed (or plantar flexed) at the end of the down-beat. The water pressure forces the foot and ankle into plantar flexion, if the ankle joint and surrounding muscles are relaxed. A pointed toe action minimises frontal resistance and allows the body to stabilise as it rotates on its horizontal axis.

Most of the kicking power originates from the hips as they flex throughout the kicking action. Muscular force originates from the big thigh muscles, creating power for the down-beat. A flutter kick with an excessive knee bend slows down the swimmer, because no force is generated from the thigh muscles. A strong, efficient kick creates lift force, allowing the swimmer to ride high in the water, minimising frontal resistance.

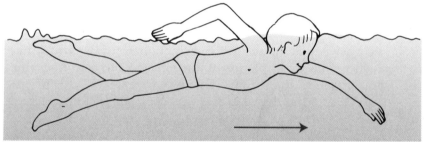

Freestyle kicking action.

Breathing

As the swimmer rotates on the horizontal axis, breathing is necessary for continuous stroking. The efficient swimmer creates a 'bow wave' in front of the head, allowing water to separate and rush off the body. The 'bow wave' produces air pockets on either side of the head, where the swimmer breathes. This gives the illusion that the swimmer is breathing under water. As the swimmer rotates, the head rolls slightly to the side and air is inhaled.

The swimmer then turns the head to the centre of the body and gradually exhales. A head which is 'off centre' will cause frontal resistance. An excessive body roll, produced when inhaling air, causes deceleration and increases frontal resistance.

Summary

A successful freestyle stroke is dependent on efficient underwater sculling actions, which provide approximately 80 per cent of the propulsion. The arm must be internally rotated (thumb down, palm facing outwards) to maximise propulsion and minimise injury. On hand entry, the hand/arm is sliced into the water to minimise turbulence and, on the hand exit, water is released by slicing the arm out. Effective sculling actions ensure that the body remains high in the water, minimising drag.

Backstroke

Resistance

The backstroke body position must be as horizontal as possible, streamlined and close to the water's surface. Like freestyle, backstroke relies on the propulsion of the arms and hands for optimal movement. The flutter kick used in backstroke also acts as a stabilising force, but the up-beat provides the drive—the reverse effect of freestyle.

An inclined body position creates frontal resistance and turbulence, due to an inefficient kick and, possibly, a fear of not being able to see the direction of travel. Successful backstroke depends on a fluent body roll to maximise the power of the upper body and a fast flutter kick to create speed and balance.

Frontal resistance is produced if the body is not horizontal and the kick is too deep, that is, exceeds a depth of 30 centimetres (12 inches). Wide, sweeping arm actions also cause resistance and turbulence.

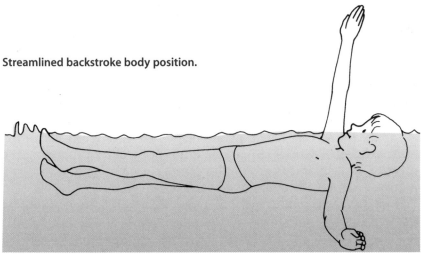

Streamlined backstroke body position.

Effective sculling movements minimise turbulence and frontal resistance. Lift force is a product of sculling to allow positive forward movement and an elevated body position to reduce drag.

Propulsion

Key considerations for efficient backstroke include the following:

1. A carefully executed hand entry is important at the start of the underwater pull-push phase. The little finger enters the water first as the arm is outstretched in the 11 o'clock position (right hand). A careful entry ensures that turbulence is reduced. Air bubbles are created around the body if the hand 'crashes' down on the water, rather than making a 'sliced and streamlined' entry. Eddy turbulence is minimised if the hand enters with control.

2. As the hand starts the catch phase, the wrist must be firm to effectively 'grip' onto the water. A good catch ensures the body is gaining significant movement. A floppy wrist is ineffective, as the swimmer loses speed at the most critical part of the stroke. The hand should travel to a depth no greater than 40 centimetres (1 foot and 4 inches) and begin the catch and pull phases. A good catch depth ensures the pull and push are maximised, allowing for the 90° arm bend to produce optimal power.

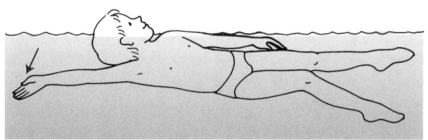

Catch phase of backstroke arm action.

3. As the hand travels through the pull phase, the elbow is bent at 90° in line with the shoulder. At this point the arm will form a 'V' shape to increase arm power. The body's leverage system—the arms and legs—works to gain maximum power by producing the greatest muscular force. Angling the arms and legs effectively increases stroke efficiency.

4. The push is a downward sweep to the thigh, with the palm of the hand facing the bottom of the pool. A long stroke ensures the body's propulsive forces are effective by gaining the greatest dis-

tance per stroke. The downward sweep creates lift force, elevating the body to ride on the water's surface. As the hand pushes against the water, it travels backwards and downwards The opposite then occurs—the body travels forwards and upwards. Gravity acts to stabilise the body at the water's surface.

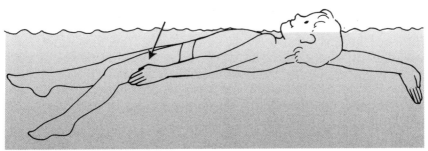

Hand exiting the water with minimal resistance.

Propulsion—Legs and Feet

The legs and feet play a crucial role in backstroke by supporting the body as the torso rotates to gain optimal power and speed. The up-beat of the backstroke kick provides the most drive as the thigh muscles contract to create force.

Plantar flexion of the feet ensures movement will be efficient. The feet also angle in towards the body's midline—a movement called *inversion*. The forces of the water allow inversion to occur naturally if the surrounding muscles are relaxed.

Summary

Efficient backstroke requires various practice drills to enhance fluency and increase stroke rate. The arm and hand speed during the underwater phase is crucial, so that maximum distance per stroke is achieved while maintaining a high stroke rate. A fluent body rotation produces maximum force from the big muscles of the upper body and is complemented by the additional drive of the strong flutter kick.

Breaststroke

Resistance

Breaststroke is the slowest competitive stroke because the arm recovery and leg recovery create frontal resistance. The underwater actions of the arms and legs cause water to hit the thighs and arms, resulting in deceleration. The high degree of resistance created in breaststroke has resulted in dramatic changes to the stroke at the highest competitive levels. The 'wave style' breaststroke produces an undulating action so that the body is riding high on the water. The dolphin-like action allows the swimmer to be elevated and to minimise frontal resistance.

The glide phase is important in elementary skill practices so that the timing of the stroke is emphasised. This helps to minimise turbulence because the body is streamlined. The feet must come together at the end of the kick to promote a streamlined body position. It is common for swimmers to continue on to the next stroke cycle without completing the propulsive phase properly. The hands-together-feet-together positions should be attained before the propulsive phase is completed.

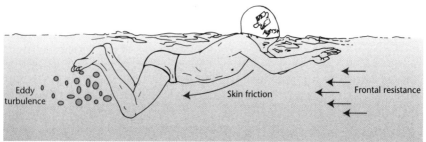

Resistance during breaststroke.

Eddy turbulence is also a problem when the heels move towards the buttocks in the leg recovery, creating swirls of disturbed water and slowing down the swimmer. A high body position and good knee flexion minimise both eddy and frontal resistance. The face should be in the water as the arms complete the recovery, so that the streamlined effect is maximised.

An elevated head during the recovery creates an inclined body position, thus increasing frontal resistance. The head carefully extends forwards as the arms start the recovery.

Propulsion

Key considerations for efficient breaststroke include the following:

1. The catch of the breaststroke arm action is important to maximise the propulsive forces of the arms and upper body. The wrists must be firm and palms face backwards and downwards as the catch starts. The hands sweep out wider than the shoulders in a sculling action. When the hand 'grips' onto the water, propulsive drag is produced, as the hand creates an axis point for the body to pass over when the arm lengthens.

2. The insweep of the arm action provides the greatest amount of lift in the stroke, allowing the upper body to rise. The shoulders come out of the water and the body is inclined. At this point air is inhaled. A breath is always taken at the point that maximum lift is produced. This minimises frontal resistance and ensures that coordination of the stroke is maintained.

3. During the insweep of the arms, the movement is accelerated using a sculling action. This maximises forward propulsion and lift. The legs also accelerate during the propulsive phase to create a 'whipping' action. The accelerated movements produce maximum power because the speed at which the muscles contract is increased. Continuous accelerated sculling actions produce constant forward movement.

4. The arm and leg recovery is usually slower than the powerful propulsive phases. They actually increase frontal resistance and create eddy turbulence around the feet and legs. The feet dorsiflex during recovery because the muscles relax to conserve energy. Dorsi flexion also places the feet in the correct position to grip onto the water in the propulsive phase. The inside of the foot and lower leg or calf catches the water, and the body travels forwards as the legs straighten.

5. In the arm recovery, the hands meet together under the chin, but they may be angled in an open or closed position—like an open book or a hands-in-prayer position. Swimmers have achieved success with both methods, although the open hand angle is better suited to the wave style technique because the hands do not create significant frontal resistance in the recovery. The teacher should encourage the method which suits the individual, depending on the efficiency of the sculling actions. The traditional closed hand position may be better suited to beginners.

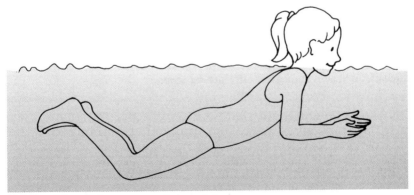

Hand position during recovery in breaststroke.

Summary

Breaststroke creates a considerable amount of drag, which has been successfully minimised by coaches who strive to find a faster alternative. Because leg and arm recovery occurs under the water, the speed of breaststroke will not significantly change. The stroke has evolved into a stroke which is close to the water's surface and is constantly undulating to create the dolphin-like action.

Butterfly

Resistance

Butterfly is like 'double arm freestyle' but is slower than freestyle because its wider outsweep and deeper knee bend create greater frontal resistance. The symmetrical arm and leg movements can cause rapid fatigue because great strength is required from the upper body for the double arm recovery.

Students need to practise dolphin-like movement—a natural undulating movement helps to produce natural speed. Various elementary drills to encourage good flexion from the hips and an efficient dolphin kick are necessary to gain effective propulsion.

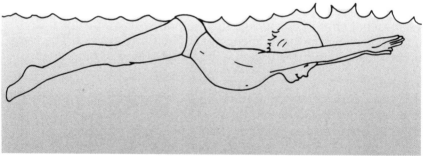

Degree of hip flexion during butterfly kicking action.

Excessive flexion of the hips and head creates frontal resistance and is a common problem with beginners. The use of fins is encouraged to help beginners achieve the undulating movement required. The head acts as a control point of the body, and any excessive head movement will cause resistance.

Propulsion

Key considerations for efficient butterfly include the following:

1. The arms glide down to a depth of 20 centimetres (8 inches) as the arms begin the outsweep. The thumbs point downwards as the palms face outwards. Effective sculling during the outsweep and insweep provides the lift that is required to breathe properly and will assist in the undulating movement of the body. The outsweep is very important in setting up a strong insweep that enhances the speed of the arm pull.

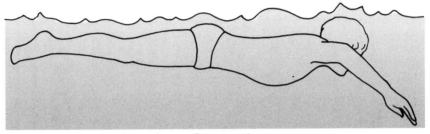

Propulsive outsweep phase of butterfly arm action.

2. The final sweep of the butterfly is referred to as the upsweep, which produces the greatest power in the arm action. This phase also produces lift and blends in with the previous insweep phase. The head breaks the surface of the water during the upsweep, and full inhalation occurs when the arms start to recover. The breath is taken when the body produces the greatest amount of lift, therefore not disrupting the natural flow of the butterfly stroke. This action prevents greater turbulence and frontal resistance.

3. The above-water arm recovery of the butterfly should cleanly enter the water, with the hands entering at 45° to minimise turbulence. A slight bent arm recovery is recommended to enable a clean entry in line with the shoulders. It is quite acceptable for swimmers to adopt a straight arm recovery, and it will work efficiently if the entry is clean and the shoulder joint speed is relatively fast.

Butterfly arm recovery.

4. The kick works in unison with the upper body so the dolphin-like action of the body is coordinated efficiently. The down-beat provides the drive and occurs as the hands enter the water and again as the hands leave the water. There must be two kicks per stroke cycle so that the stroke maintains acceleration. Like freestyle and backstroke, the kick must originate from the hips to produce maximum force. The knees simply bend to assist in the body's undulating action. As the hands enter the water, the buttocks come out of the water because the hips flex to assist in the dolphin-like action.

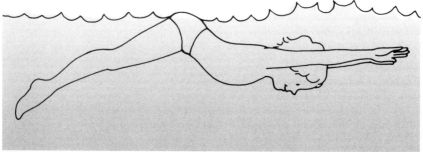

Buttocks at surface of water as the arm action commences.

Propulsion—Legs and Feet

The legs work in symmetry to produce efficient movement. The dolphin kick has been proven to be the most effective underwater kick because the paired leg action creates less turbulence. As in freestyle, the down-beat provides the drive, but the knee bend is slightly deeper to promote the undulating action and to provide greater stability as the arms exit and recover. Good hip flexion is the key to an efficient kick, and the legs should be allowed to move naturally from the undulating movement of the upper body.

Summary

The butterfly stroke has evolved in recent years as coaches have attempted to break records by encouraging swimmers to travel under water for a long distance. (Federation Internationale de Natation Amateur rules limit the distance to a maximum of 15 metres [49 feet and 2 inches].) Turbulence and eddies are created when the body is on the surface and more splash is produced.

Swimming underwater minimises these resistances, but only an extremely effective kick will produce good speed. After a freestyle tumbleturn, the dolphin kick is used instead of the flutter kick. As humans have studied the efficient movements of marine life, they have adopted the improved techniques to increase speed. The butterfly stroke is a classic example: It aims to simulate the movement patterns of the dolphin.

Sidestroke

Resistance

The sidestroke is the only stroke in which the body is on its side. The body position is streamlined, on its side, with the lower arm extended beyond the head.

As one arm recovers and the legs adopt the scissors kick action, significant frontal resistance is created. The wide, sweeping action of the legs in the recovery phase creates a slow stroke, but the fast 'snapping' action of the legs in the propulsive phase produces good speed.

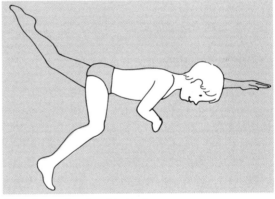

Wide leg action for sidestroke.

The arms work in unison, one arm always providing propulsion as the other arm recovers. As in the lifesaving backstroke, the recovering arm 'slides' through the water to minimise eddies and frontal resistance. The effective sculling actions of the arms and hands attempt to maximise forward movement, but this can happen only when there is no victim in tow.

Propulsion

Key considerations for efficient sidestroke include the following:

1. The elbows bend in the propulsive phases of both arms to generate maximum power, assisting the legs to increase speed. The face of each hand opens to effectively catch the water and propel

the body forwards. When the hands open up to 'grip' the water, it results in positive drag. As the arms extend, the body travels past the point where the water was caught.

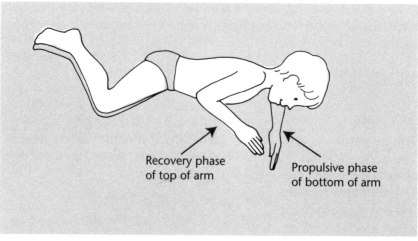

Recovery phase
of top of arm

Propulsive phase
of bottom of arm

Sidestroke arm action.

2. The powerful closure of the legs in the propulsive phase of the scissors kick is the source of optimal movement in the stroke. The top leg (i.e. the leg closest to the surface of the water) comes forwards and the foot is dorsiflexed. The back of the top leg and the sole of the foot catch the water and propel the body forward. The bottom leg flexes from the knee, and the toe is angled away from the body. The toe is pointed (plantar flexed), producing a strong hold on the water to maximise propulsion.

3. If the arm action and leg action fail to coordinate, the stroke will create turbulence because the struggle to synchronise the stroke will produce disturbed water. To improve coordination the arm action can be performed with just one arm working with the legs, and land drills of the action can be practised.

4. The glide phase is streamlined, with the bottom arm extended and the top arm positioned on the thigh. The head must rest on the water's surface, with the cheek and ear in the water. A raised head produces an inclined body position, which will increase frontal resistance. It can also cause turbulence because the angle of the legs will produce an ineffective kick. The body must travel in the horizontal plane to prevent further resistance.

Survival Backstroke

Resistance

The survival strokes encounter greater resistance than the competitive strokes because of underwater recovery actions. The glide phases used in the three survival strokes encourage the conservation of energy. However, efficient arm and leg actions can speed up rescues and assist with the stabilisation of the victim.

Like the breaststroke, the survival backstroke causes considerable frontal resistance due to the kicking action. The lifesaving backstroke kick is the reverse copy of the breaststroke kick. The body position is horizontal, with the back on the water's surface, and the swimmer is encouraged to keep as close to the water's surface as possible. The sculling actions of the arms also create significant frontal resistance and turbulence. The sweeping action of the hands during arm recovery causes deceleration.

Propulsion

Key considerations for efficient survival backstroke are as follows:

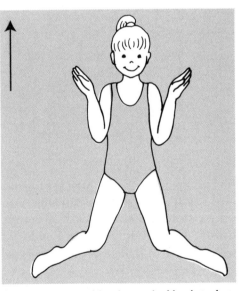

1. The arm recovery will create frontal resistance, but if the hands 'slide' through the water towards the shoulders, it will minimise resistance. The arm can be compared to an oar, the blade of which is the hand. Opening the face of the hand produces maximum speed in the propulsive phase of the arm action, and the hand changes its angle during the recovery phase—exactly the same action as the oar.

Arm recovery position in survival backstroke.

2. The hands finish next to the thighs at the end of the push to maximise distance per stroke and to encourage streamlining in the glide phase. The elbows bend during the propulsive phase to maximise the power generated from the upper body. The paired arm

action in the propulsive phase can be compared to the backstroke action, but the hands do not extend far beyond the shoulders in the survival backstroke.

3. The leg action starts with a bend at the knee joint to drop the lower legs (leg recovery) to set up the propulsive phase. It is common for beginners to flex their hips so the knees break the water. This action increases frontal resistance and causes eddy turbulence to form around the legs close to the water's surface. If this action occurs, the body position will incline and result in an inefficient movement.

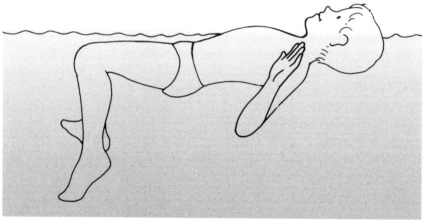

Propulsive phase of survival backstroke.

4. When the lower legs are dropped, ready for the propulsive phase, the ankles dorsiflex and are positioned to 'grab' the water, and the legs extend and follow a semicircular path to maximise propulsion. It is important to realise that the leg rotation comes from the hip and not the knee. The knees start the propulsive action 30 centimetres (12 inches) apart, which assists the lower legs to rotate efficiently.

5. The legs finish in an extended position for a streamlined glide phase. The toes are pointed (plantar flexed) to minimise frontal resistance. The stroke cycle continues.

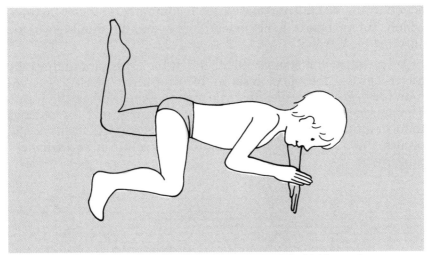

Leg position in survival backstroke at the beginning of the kicking action.

Chapter 5

INTRODUCING DIVING TO BEGINNERS

During the water familiarisation phase the beginner is exposed to numerous underwater activities involving breath holding, placing the head under the water and taking the feet from the bottom and recovering confidently. Water entry experiences, including tumbling, rolling and jumping into water, will also prepare students for diving or an entry with hands first, then head and then the rest of the body.

After these introductory experiences it is time to develop beginners' competency in more advanced entry skills to provide a sound base for recreational activities and competitive swimming and diving. During learn-to-swim classes, rather than jumping or diving, students should enter the water using the slide-in method when asked to demonstrate strokes.

Diving for beginners.

Diving and jumping are the two acceptable methods of entry into the water by recreational swimmers. They are complex entries, and students require an understanding of the various safety factors to significantly reduce the risk of serious spinal injury.

When learning to dive from the edge of flush level pools, the inexperienced diver should be taught in water at least the depth of the learner's vertically raised arms. Experienced divers should practise in water that is at least the depth of their horizontally stretched arms. When diving from starting blocks, experienced or trained competitive swimmers may perform dives into water with a minimum depth of 1.2 metres (3 feet and 11 inches).

The Dangers of Diving

It is hoped that the 'macho' attraction of diving that results in so many serious spinal injuries for young males can be reduced by discouraging diving from any place that is not specifically designed for diving.

For a diver to enter the water safely hands first, followed by the arms, head, trunk and legs, a number of factors need to be considered:

- The height of the entry
- The depth of the water
- The height and weight of the diver
- The angle of the entry
- The type of dive
- What the diver does under the water (e.g. keeps the hands locked in front of the head, angles up, raises the head).

Dive only from diving platforms where the depth of the water is known.

The complex calculations required to judge whether it is safe to dive are beyond most teenagers. While a jumping entry can still result in serious injury, the type of injury sustained is less likely to result in quadriplegia. Teenagers will continue to take risks, and it is the responsibility of swimming and water safety teachers to properly inform them of the dangers and to discourage them from performing dangerous activities. If it is essential to enter the water from a height greater than 0.75 metre (2.46 feet), the main message is 'Jump, don't dive'.

Diving in the natural environment can be dangerous.

Rules for Safe Entry

The following safety rules indicate the level of information required to assess a safe entry. (It is recommended that teachers encourage alternative, safer entries.):

- Never dive or slide head first into shallow water (i.e. where the depth is less than the person's length when her or his arms are extended vertically).
- Recreational swimmers should perform only shallow dives (i.e. no deeper than 50 centimetres [1 foot and 8 inches] under the surface of the water).
- Do not perform a shallow dive from a height greater than .75 metre (2 feet and 6 inches).
- Do not dive from structures not specifically designed for diving.

- After entry, hold the head and arms up and aim for the surface.
- Always keep hands locked together and stretched in front of the head.
- Do not run and dive.
- Do not dive across the narrow part of a pool—it is safer to dive from the end.
- Do back dives or competition dives only from diving boards or diving platforms.
- Platform diving should always be taught and supervised by a qualified diving coach.
- Slide in to check the water depth before diving or jumping into unfamiliar bodies of water.
- Check for 'No diving' or 'No jumping' signs and obey them.
- If diving or jumping into naturally occurring bodies of water, check regularly for changes in depth or water conditions.

Children enjoy jumping and diving into the water, so they must learn correct techniques when they are capable of performing them. It is vitally important to highlight the dangers of entries when teaching children to swim.

Swimmers must be aware of the dangers of diving into unknown pools, ponds, dams, rivers or creeks.

Teaching Diving as an Entry

Contrary to previous practice, AUSTSWIM does not now endorse the teaching of deep dives. It is not appropriate for swimming instructors to teach vertical entries for recreational diving to beginner divers. Diving over a barrel or through a hoop should be taught only by qualified diving instructors, as these activities encourage a vertical entry. AUSTSWIM encourages the teaching of the shallow dive. The same principles apply to the shallow dive as to the glide, and the shallow dive should be developed as a glide entry from the side. The head should be kept in a neutral position, neither chin in nor head back. More experienced divers can develop the shallow dive to a maximum angle of 30° but should not attempt it from heights greater than .75 metre (2 feet and 6 inches).

Teaching the Forward Dive

Step 1. Surface Glide

The teacher should position students in the waist-deep section of the pool with their backs to the poolside. With faces down in the water and using one or both feet, students push off from the side, gliding on the water's surface with arms and legs fully extended and hands locked together in front. Remind them to keep their eyes open under the water.

The hands should then be pulled down and under the body and, at the same time, the knees brought forward and the feet placed on the bottom of the pool. During this action, the heads are raised. The students are now standing upright in the water.

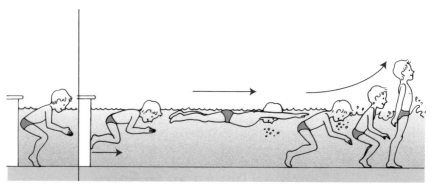

Surface glide.

Step 2. Crouch Position (Sit Dive)

Sit students on the poolside, equally spaced to allow free body movement.

They place their feet on the rail or edge of the pool, drawing their knees up to the chest and under the chin. The arms should be extended in front with hands clasped together and touching the water. The head is held up.

They then push from the side, arms extended and hands locked together and head up, into the water.

This skill practice should be repeated until students enter the water competently.

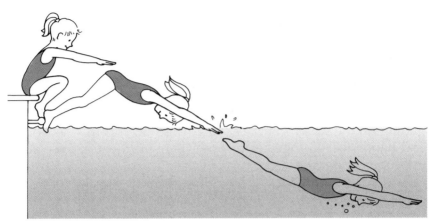

Diving from the edge of a pool.

Step 3. Standing Position—Semi-Crouch

Students stand on the deck of the pool with toes curled over the edge, the knees bent and the feet slightly apart to maintain balance.

They fall towards the water and then straighten their legs, pushing back against the edge of the pool and projecting their bodies forwards and their legs upwards. As their bodies rotate in the air, their hands enter the water first, followed by the rest of their bodies, held in a streamlined position. The angle of entry can vary from parallel to a maximum of 30°.

Following entry, students aim their hands towards the surface and lift their heads. Their hands must remain locked together in front of their heads throughout the dive.

Diving from a standing position.

Chapter 6

TOWARDS EFFICIENT STROKE DEVELOPMENT

Common Strokes

The following are some of the competitive and survival swimming strokes commonly used throughout the world.

Freestyle

Freestyle as it is known today originated as the 'Australian crawl' or 'front crawl'. Vast improvements and increases in swimming speed have been seen with the refinement of the stroke.

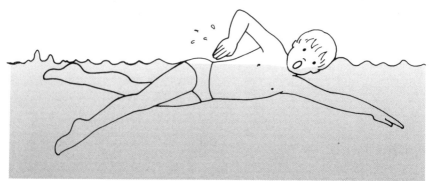

Freestyle.

Backstroke

The backstroke developed from the basic back float as people sought mobility while floating on their backs.

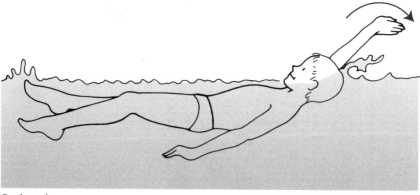

Backstroke.

Breaststroke

The breaststroke was the method first used to move the body in water. It is still taught today as the basis and basic stroke for all swimming.

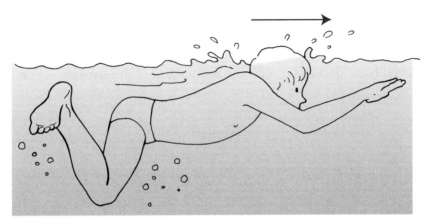

Breaststroke.

Butterfly

The breaststroke developed into the stroke now known as the butterfly through competitions—breaststrokers were looking to improve the speed of the stroke. Officials established the butterfly stroke as a competitive stroke and tightened the rules on breaststroke to prevent any form of above-water recovery.

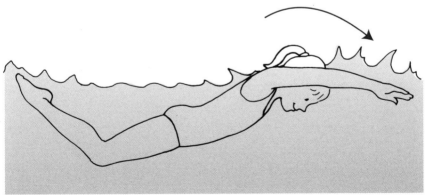

Butterfly.

Sidestroke

The sidestroke is a useful technique for both personal survival and the rescue of others. It is particularly suitable for rescues because breathing and kicking actions are not hindered during towing.

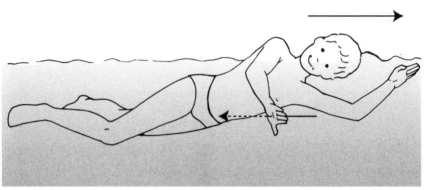

Sidestroke.

Survival Backstroke

The survival backstroke is effective in both rescue and survival situations. The face is clear of the water, so breathing is uninterrupted, and the inverted 'frog' or 'whip' kick is an efficient means of propulsion.

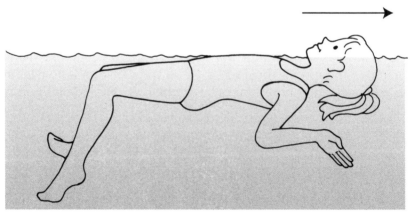

Survival backstroke.

Stroke Characteristics

Each stroke offers various advantages and is appropriate for various purposes.

Freestyle
- competition
- rescue
- recreation
- water polo

Backstroke
- competition
- recreation
- water polo

Breaststroke
- competition
- rescue
- survival
- recreation
- water polo

Butterfly
- competition
- prone board paddling

Sidestroke
- competition
- rescue
- recreation
- survival
- water polo

Survival backstroke
- competition
- rescue
- recreation
- survival

Each of the strokes may be introduced to beginners in any order, depending on individual circumstances. The objective of any instruction in strokes is to improve the mobility of beginners and increase their awareness of water safety. The development of appropriate and efficient skills is important to all learners. Many of these basic skills are useful for learning all strokes.

The sequencing of skills is important—correct sequencing results in a faster and more effective learning process. The development of these skills must be based on an individual's own learning response and should be programmed to suit each individual beginner.

Swimming Basics

Key Skills

Mobility is the goal for beginner swimmers. To achieve a high level of mobility in the aquatic environment, beginners must develop the basic skills of water confidence, streamlining, recovery and propulsion.

These skills need to be taught in an easy-to-remember sequence that can be adopted as a basis for all swimming strokes. The sequence, once learned, can then be the foundation for all future stroke development and can be reinforced as the strokes are further developed and refined. These basic mobility skills are of immense value to swimmers at all levels of stroke development up through competitive swimming and lifesaving.

The sequence that can be taught and retained at a young age is simple: submerge the face, push-glide, kick, arm stroke action and recovery. Breathing skills can be included at a later stage.

These skills must be taught and reinforced to create mobile swimmers who can then develop other skills which may be modified, adapted and refined as required.

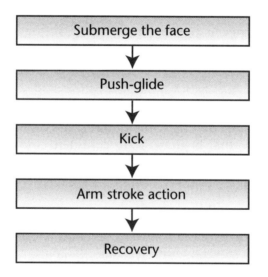

Stroke technique sequence.

These key learner skills (known as the basic learner sequence) are the basis for successful skill development and must be taught in an effective manner to result in a sound base of skill learning by beginners.

During the initial stroke development phase, beginners should experiment with three types of body positions:

- Face down

- Face up on back

- Face on side

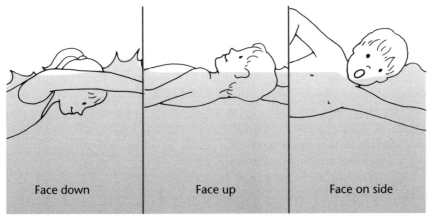

| Face down | Face up | Face on side |

Three types of body position.

Face Immersion

While this skill is often one of the most difficult for beginners to acquire, time spent on teaching this skill is extremely valuable at all future learning stages. This skill must be practised in a variety of different water depths, temperatures and conditions (if available) to ensure that beginners are confident and that they have learned the skill effectively. Activities used to introduce and develop this skill are explained in chapter 2.

Face-Down Gliding Position—Start

The means of developing a streamlined body position commences with beginners standing with feet slightly apart and knees bent to allow the shoulders to be under the water. The chin rests on the surface of the water and the arms extend forwards, shoulder-width apart.

Starting position for a face-down glide.

Glide

Beginners take in a 'normal' volume of air and place the head into the water until approximately one-third of the skull area is in the water and the face is looking down and slightly forwards. They push gently from the bottom into a streamlined position, indicated by the buttocks and the heels at the surface of the water. If the heels are not at the surface, the head should be pressed a little deeper into the water. Beginners can also practise the glide by placing one foot against the wall of the pool and pushing off.

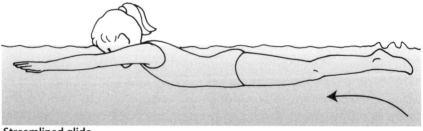

Streamlined glide.

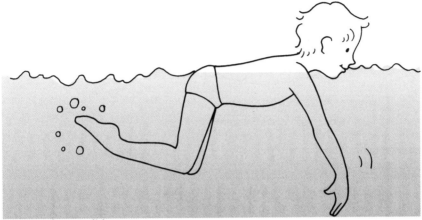

Recovery from a glide.

Recovery

Following the glide, beginners should press the hands towards the bottom of the water while drawing the knees to the chest into a tuck position. The head should exit the water following the completion of the tucking action.

Face Up—Back Float

This skill is taught once beginners are confident in performing the face-down body position.

Gliding Position—Start

Beginners stand with feet together and bend the knees to lower the shoulders into the water with chin at water level.

Starting position for back glide.

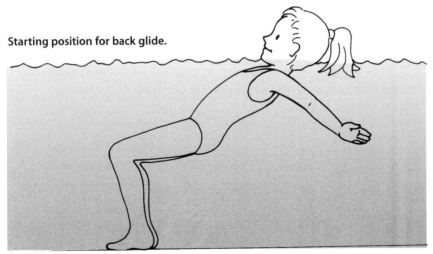

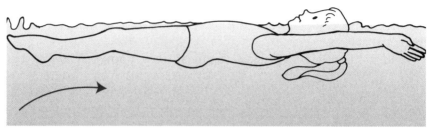

Back glide position.

Glide

The glide is commenced by pushing off gently, with the ears just under the surface and the eyes looking upwards.

Recovery

Following the glide the knees are drawn towards the chest while the head is brought towards the knees.

Face on the Side

The body-on-side position is relatively easy to perform once beginners are competent at both the face downward and face upward body positions. Beginners should concentrate on keeping the lower ear on the surface of the water as they practise the glide.

Constant attention to the development of natural breathing patterns should be given throughout the learning of the body position and leg kicking actions. Attention to correct breathing techniques continues when the respective arm actions are being taught.

Glide With Kick

Following the acquisition of a streamlined body position, beginners may progress to propelling activities by kicking the legs. Beginners should be encouraged to practise both competitive and survival kicking actions. The kick is a continuous action.

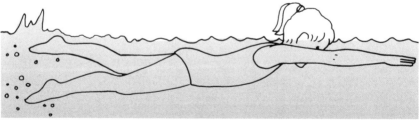

Kicking action with streamlined body position.

When initial practices for breaststroke and butterfly are being performed, the push from the bottom should commence with the feet together to encourage the development of the desired symmetrical action.

Information on all main swimming strokes follows. At the end of each 'stroke section' you will find specific teaching progressions about that stroke. Suggested steps are supported by notes made in point form in order to provide a simple, quick reference for teachers.

Many drills have gained acceptance in developing particular aspects of the strokes. The drills listed in the 'Suggested Steps' are tried, tested and known to be effective. However, many other drills and strategies can be employed successfully.

In order to avoid confusing students when moving from one class to another, it is recommended that a common approach to the introduction of progressive drills and skills should be adopted by all teachers within an individual program.

Freestyle

Once the basic learner sequence has been developed and the skill of kick and recovery has been taught, then the skills of stroke and breathing can be introduced.

Leg Action

The common term for the freestyle kick is the *flutter kick*, as the feet appear to flutter at the surface. The legs should be relaxed and the movement begun at the top of the legs. The leg flexes slightly at the knee on the down-beat and then straightens on the up-beat.

Plantar flexion of the feet (toe moves away from shin, like a ballet dancer on points) is important in the freestyle kick, but it should be the pressure of the water that plantar flexes the foot, not the straining of the swimmer. The action should be continuous.

Arm Action

Before actually teaching the freestyle arm action it is important for teachers to have a sound understanding of the correct technique and its components.

Entry

- The hand entry must be smooth, with a high wrist and elbow action.
- Entry should be made approximately on the 'shoulder line'.
- The index finger and thumb should enter the water first.

After the entry, the hand slides forwards and slightly downwards. As the elbow reaches the extended position, the opposite hand is completing its propulsive pushing action.

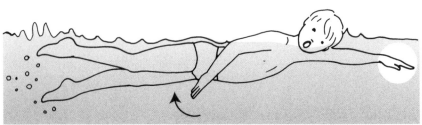

Hand position after entry.

Catch

- The catch is made following entry of the hand.
- The catch is performed with the wrist slightly flexed.
- The little finger leads the hand in a slight outward sweep, which applies force against the water and propels the body forwards.

The entry and catch components are considered by many to be the most important aspects of the stroke.

Position of the hand as it catches the water.

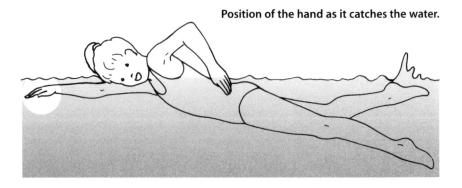

Pull

- At the completion of the catch, the elbow has begun to flex and the hand begins a downward and outward pathway.
- The elbow continues to flex during the downsweep.
- As the hand approaches its deepest point, the downsweep is rounded off into an insweep, with the elbow flexed to right angles and the arm under the shoulders.

Push

- The push phase commences at the end of the insweep.
- During the propulsive push phase, the hand moves outwards and upwards.
- The hand does not move backwards but propels the body forwards.
- Once the hip has moved over the hand, pressure against the palm of the hand is released and the elbow begins to flex to allow the hand to leave the water smoothly.

S-shaped movement pathway of hand.

The push phase is the most propulsive part of the arm stroke.

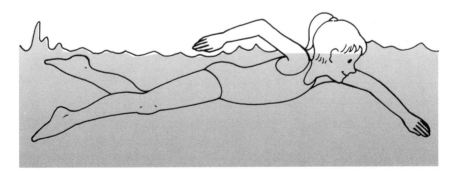

Pull.

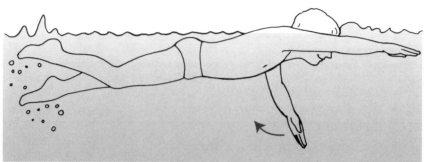

Position of the hand at the start of push phase.

Recovery

- The desired arm recovery is with a high elbow action initiated by a roll of the shoulder with the hands passing close to the sides of the body.
- The recovery commences at the end of the upward push movement of the hand.
- The hand travels upwards, slightly outwards and forwards during the first half of the recovery with the palm facing either inwards or backwards.
- The arm then extends forwards and downwards as the index finger and thumb slide gracefully into the water for the catch.

The whole-skill teaching method is the best to use when introducing arm strokes. Only when beginners have difficulty with skills or require further development should the skill be taught in individual parts.

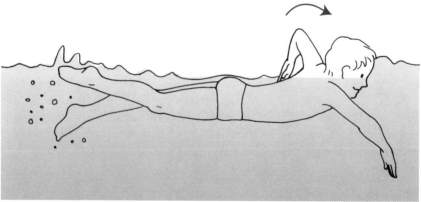

Bent arm during above-water recovery.

Stroke Practices for Advanced Beginners

Power Stroke Practice

The power stroke is a continuous arm stroke style for which the arms move almost opposite to each other. When one arm is in front, the other is at the back. At no time should both hands be seen in front of the head. A six-, four-, or two-beat kick rhythm may be used. Students should practise counting half the chosen number of kicks for each arm movement. Encourage students to practise short distances at first, with the face in all the time. Later, they can practise over longer distances, adding breathing.

High Elbow Practice

Often called 'Chicken Wings', this drill is used to develop a high elbow style. On recovery, the elbow is lifted high, with the thumb drawn along the side of the body until the thumb reaches the armpit. The fingers should be relaxed. This practice can also be done with the back of the hand and fingertips trailing along the surface of the water.

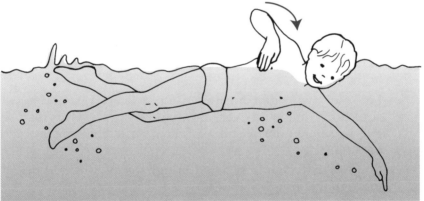

High elbow practice.

Evaluating Technique

Look for the features listed here. The overall timing, or flow, of the stroke is more important than the precision of details. Remember, an individual's success in freestyle depends on the following:

- Smoothness as one arm takes over from the other for each pull
- 'High in the water' body position
- Good body alignment, first on one side, then on the other

- Balanced movements (right arm same as the left, same amount of bend, etc.)
- Good head position and ease of breathing to either side
- Economical use of legs

The following freestyle performance criteria have been identified as essential elements in an efficient stroke.

Body positions

- During the stroke, check that the body rotates on its side with one shoulder much higher than the other.
- Look for controlled body-tilting or rolling, with shoulders rolling the same amount to each side.
- Emphasise that shoulders are not held flat.

Basic head positions

- Look for an upward curve of the neck, the head tilted so the waterline is about at the hairline.
- Emphasise that the head follows the body roll and remains in a comfortable, restful position. There should be no sudden jerks of the head.

Breathing

- Emphasise that breathing adds merely a few degrees of roll to the head, exposing the mouth to the air in the natural dip in the water.
- Look for two-sided breathing—once every one-and-a-half strokes, in time with every third arm recovery. (This may be taught later, after beginners have mastered single-sided breathing.)
- Emphasise that air is inhaled through the mouth and exhaled through the mouth and nose.
- Emphasise that breath flows out and is *not blown out*. Also, beginners *must not hold their breath*.
- The timing must be coordinated so that when the swimmer is breathing on the right, the sequence commences when the left arm enters the water; when the swimmer is breathing on the left, the right arm entry triggers the breath.

Leg action

- Look for continuous kicking action.
- Emphasise that the kick originates from the hips.

- See that the legs are relaxed and the ankles are plantar flexed but loose.
- Watch that legs are slightly bent on the down-beat but straight on the up-beat.

Arm action

- Emphasise that hands are *not excessively cupped*, as it is preferable that fingers be held loosely together, creating a paddle.
- For the arm entry, look for fingers entering first, followed by the wrist, the forearm and then the elbow. See that the thumb side of the hand is tilted slightly lower than the little-finger side.
- The hand should enter on the shoulder line. Emphasise that the arm pull starts slowly and gradually speeds up, with the arm looking as though it is curving downwards 'over a barrel'. The upper arm stays near the top of the water, then joins as a pulling surface. In the middle of the pull, the elbow points to the side of the pool. The hand makes an 'S' during the pull. See that the pull ends prior to full extension and that the thumb grazes the thigh as the hand moves into the recovery phase.
- Ensure that the hand does not cross the midline of the body.

Recovery

- For the recovery, watch that the shoulder appears first above the surface, followed by the upper arm, elbow, wrist and hand. See that the elbow is lifted high and the forearm swings around loosely. The fingers then lead as the forearm is aimed to the re-entry point.
- Emphasise that the forearm and hand are completely relaxed through all but the final positioning for the re-entry.

Timing

- Note that it is the timing of the arm movements relative to each other that sets the two standard styles of freestyle apart.
- In the semi-catch-up freestyle, emphasise that one arm moves through the last half of its pull, its entire recovery, then enters in front while the other arm moves through only the first half of the pull.
- In the power stroke freestyle, emphasise that there is little or no pause or glide of the hand in front. One arm enters barely in time to take over pulling before the other arm finishes the push.

The arm action is first introduced to beginners as a complete action (it is important not to over-analyse the skill at the point of introduction).

Beginners are encouraged to make large arm circles during the start of the arm action learning phase. As students gain confidence and skill, practices can be introduced to enable movement patterns of the 'technically correct' competitive stroke to be developed. Initial practices of the arm movement may take place on land prior to beginners entering the water. Following walking practice, the arm action can be developed with beginners in the prone gliding position. A kickboard may be used during the gliding practices when the arm action is being taught.

There is a school of thought that the technically correct arm action should be taught from the outset. However, most people believe that the technically correct action is far too complex a skill for beginners to master and the learning of the arm action through a sequence of practices is the preferred option.

Beginners often rush the arm action, usually because they do not feel confident lifting an arm out of the water. They must be reminded to practise continuous, slow strokes which take advantage of the body's natural buoyancy. This often needs to be reinforced every lesson, especially with young beginners.

Breathing Practice

Timing

Before the timing of the arm action to the breathing pattern can be taught, it is essential that beginners develop an efficient breathing movement pattern. The following drills may assist.
Beginners

- hold a kickboard with one hand, thumb underneath and the fingers on top and elbow extended.
- bend the knees to allow the shoulders to be under the water, turn the head to the side and place the face flat onto the water.

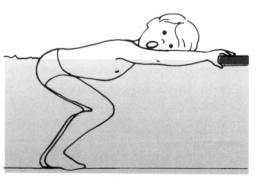

Breathing to the side in a stationary position.

- breathe in naturally and gently rotate the head until the eyes are facing the bottom of the pool. Without a pause they gently rotate the head out again.

During the inward and outward rotation, exhalation should occur through the mouth and nose.

Practise this drill while walking across the pool.

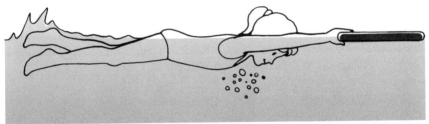

Practise this drill while kicking across the pool.

Using a kickboard, beginners do a catch-up stroke. Each time the hand reaches the board to replace the other hand, beginners should lean on that hand and immediately turn the head to the opposite side to take a breath (inhale). They then complete another stroke cycle before repeating the sequence.

This activity promotes a relaxed and early breathing sequence that can be adapted to suit each individual.

When introducing breathing timing, many teachers ask beginners to count the strokes and then turn the head to breathe. A common method of teaching bilateral breathing had beginners count 1–2–3 and then turn the head to breathe, then count 1–2–3 and continue in that sequence. However, this method develops late breathing and should be avoided.

A more efficient method is to have beginners count 1-2 as each arm enters the water and, as the arm enters for the third stroke, turn the head for the breath (i.e. 1–2–breathe, 1–2–breathe).

Checklist for Evaluating Beginner Freestyle

❑ Relatively straight arms during pull and recovery phase

❑ Continuous arm motion

❑ Hands held relaxed

❑ Breathing as required—promote extended breathing

❑ Alternate-side (bilateral) breathing encouraged

❑ Continuous kicking

Basic Stroke Drills for Beginners

Body Rotation Practice

The body should rotate on its long axis as it moves forwards through the water. The following practices are designed to teach beginners to rotate. These activities should not be attempted until beginners are streamlined and strong in their kicking. This will have developed from previous practices.

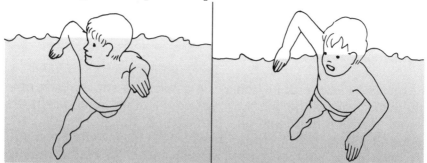

Body rotation in freestyle, highlighting high elbow recovery and bent arm pull.

Side Kick Practice

Beginners try freestyle kicking, lying on the side, one arm in front just below the surface, ear on that shoulder and the other hand still by the side. They kick in a freestyle action sideways for a short distance (10 to 25 metres [33 to 82 feet]). Beginners practise on alternate sides, changing at each end or side of the pool. During the kicking action, the knees should pass each other.

Six-Six Practice

Beginners lie on the left side as stated previously; after six kicks they rotate onto the right side while making an underwater stroke with the left hand, exhaling as the face goes under and making a 'Chicken Wing' (high elbow) recovery with the right arm. Any combination of less than six can also be used (e.g. 3:3).

Timing Drills

Catch-Up Stroke Practice

The beginner holds one hand extended in front while the other arm completes a stroke, accompanied by continuous kicking of the legs. An endless number of patterns may be used. A kickboard can be held out in front.

Here are some variations:

- The same arm is used all the time.
- Left and right arms are used alternately.
- Three left and three right arm strokes are used alternately.

The catch-up drill should not be used in excess. It is useful for beginners to develop the breathing timing. However, teachers should not allow them to become dependent on this drill to develop their swimming style.

Semi-Catch-Up Stroke Practice

In the semi-catch-up stroke practice, one hand is held extended in front until the recovery hand comes forwards as far as the elbow of the front arm. Then the gliding hand commences an arm pull, while the other hand rests in the glide position.

Continuous kicking is important in the semi-catch-up timing. The arm strokes should be slowed down in front so that there can be an acceleration as the hand moves through the underwater stroke.

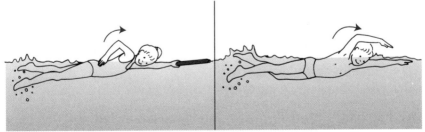

Catch-up stroke practice.   Semi-catch-up stroke practice.

Progressions

The following steps support the initial teaching of freestyle with breathing in a regular pattern. Bilateral breathing may be introduced once the stroke has been learnt, although some teachers wish to introduce bilateral breathing from the outset. Catch-up drills are used to slow the stroke and allow beginners to concentrate on one arm, promote the development of a long stroke and avoid 'over-reaching' of the hands at entry.

Kickboards, when used in the progressions, are primarily intended to be a target for the hands and should be held at the back with the fingers over and the thumb under to promote the correct hand position on entry.

Suggested Steps

1. Glide and recovery

From a gliding position (shoulders under, arms forwards):

- Horizontal body position
- Head submerged to the hairline
- Exhaling in the water
- Recovery to a standing position

2. Glide with kick

From a gliding position:

- Head submerged to the hairline
- Horizontal body position
- Exhaling in the water
- Continuous kicking

Kicking should be practised until it is effective in supporting a streamlined, horizontal body position.

3. Glide and kick with arm action

From a gliding position:

- Gliding and kicking before adding the arm action
- Exhaling in the water
- Four or five strokes per repetition

An alternating arm action without breathing is included at this stage to establish the whole skill. Some teachers prefer to omit this step.

4. Whole stroke

Alternating arm action:

- Gliding and kicking before adding the arm action
- Regular breathing on the preferred side
- Turning (not lifting) the head to breathe as required

Return to starting from a gliding position once breathing is learnt. Teachers may introduce bilateral breathing now.

- Combine bilateral breathing with arm action.
- Emphasise the rhythm ('1–2–breathe') with the entry of each arm.

Beginners accustomed to regular breathing may tend to exhale too completely prior to the second arm pull and may be assisted if they partially hold the breath during the early stage of the sequence.

Some teachers prefer to introduce bilateral breathing to a catch-up stroke, which may be promoted by the use of a board.

5. Stroke refinement

Backstroke

Once beginners have developed confidence in gliding on the back, emphasise a streamlined body position, with the body slightly angled in the water.

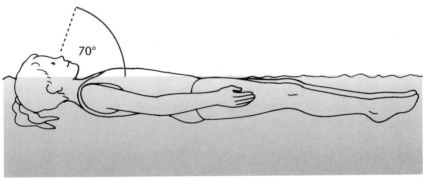

Backstroke body position.

To a large extent, the depth of the head determines the position of the body. For beginners, the ears should be just under the surface, eyes looking up at about a 70° angle and the body 'straight' and relaxed.

Kick

Beginners must keep a continuous kick action going while learning the stroke. When students practise the kick, the toes should make a 'splash' on the surface, while the knees remain below.

The feet should not be too stiff, as ankle flexibility is very important. The toes should be turned naturally inwards and a low splash kick performed. The knees flex very slightly on the down-beat and straighten on the up-beat.

Kicking Practices

Beginners may use a sculling action with the hands while initial kicking practices are being performed. Once reasonable propulsion is being obtained, a kickboard may be held to practise the action.

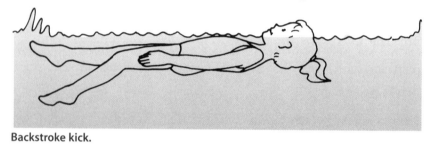

Backstroke kick.

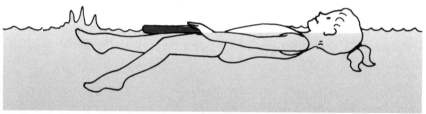

Backstroke kick, holding board over knees to promote correct action.

Breathing

While initial kicking practices are being performed, beginners should be encouraged to breathe as naturally as possible and to avoid holding the breath.

Arm Action

The whole-skill teaching method is again the best method to introduce the arm stroke. Only after beginners are experiencing difficulty should the skill be taught in individual parts.

The initial description of the arm action may be referred to as a down–up–down recovery action.

While the student performs the arm stroke, the body should not be rigid in the water but should rotate smoothly from side to side to assist the entry and recovery of the hands and arms.

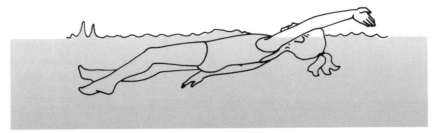

Arm entry of backstroke, with little finger entering water first.

The entry into the water is made little-finger first (palm outwards) at an 11 o'clock right-hand and a 1 o'clock left-hand position. The entry should be smooth with a minimal amount of turbulence being created. It is important that beginners do not over-reach to keep the body in a streamlined position.

Following entry, the arm remains straight and sweeps downwards and outwards to a depth of approximately 40 centimetres (1 foot and 4 inches).

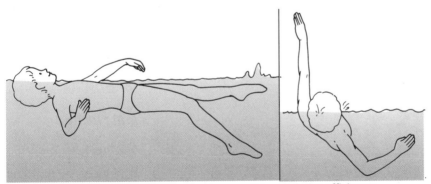

Backstroke arm pull, demonstrating bent arm pull to maximise efficiency.

Also, following the entry, the hand rotates in a rounded and upward pitch as the elbow begins to flex and pressure is applied to the palm of the hand. The ability to catch the water is considered to be the most important aspect of the stroke. The elbow continues to flex until it is bent to approximately a 90° angle at the end of the pulling action and the fingertips are relatively close to the surface of the water.

During this upward, backward and inward movement the hand should begin to accelerate.

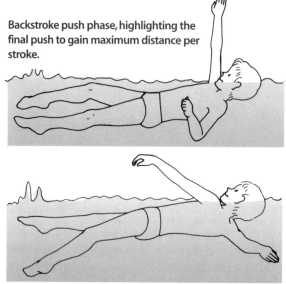

Backstroke push phase, highlighting the final push to gain maximum distance per stroke.

Arm recovery of backstroke, demonstrating a relaxed and extended arm.

Once the shoulder is level with the hand, the palm begins a downward and outward movement until the hip passes the hand. The palm finishes the propulsive phase by facing the bottom of the pool.

The shoulder lifts, followed by the arm and then the hand. The back of the hand of the recovery arm is uppermost as the hand leaves the water.

When the recovery arm reaches the vertical position, the palm faces outwards ready for a smooth, turbulence-free re-entry with the hand entering little finger first.

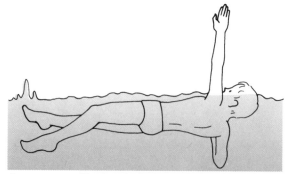

Arm recovery of backstroke in the vertical position. The palm faces outward to prepare for a turbulence-free entry.

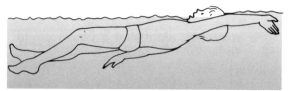

Recovery arm enters water, little finger first, as opposite arm completes propulsive phase.

Basic Practices for Beginners

Arm Practices

One-Arm Practice

Beginners swim using one arm only over the practice distance. The hand should be rotated during the recovery so that the little finger enters first, palm facing outwards. They continue until the hand is at a depth of 30 centimetres (12 inches).

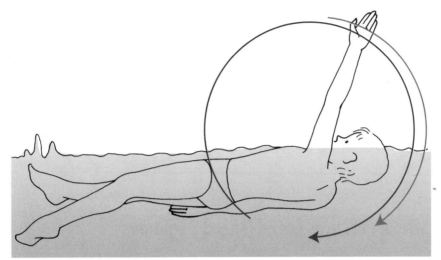

Backstroke one-arm practice.

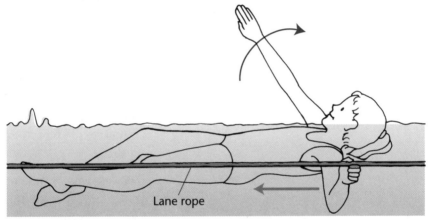

Lane rope

Lane rope practice.

Allow beginners to complete the underwater stroke without further direction at this time. Remember that the objective of the one-arm drill at this stage is to make the link between recovery, entry and catch.

Propulsion Practices

Lane Rope Practice

Beginners swim, using one arm only, alongside a lane rope (or handrail), grasping the rope with an undergrip to pull and push the body along. This practice aims to develop the desirable arm movement of bending and then straightening in the underwater stroke.

Checklist for Evaluating Beginner Backstroke

- ❑ Head back, chest up, streamlined position
- ❑ Continuous kicking and arm action
- ❑ Breathing naturally (ideally breathing in on the recovery of one arm and out on the recovery of the other arm)
- ❑ Arm recovery commencing with the little finger leading
- ❑ Relatively straight arms during the recovery phase
- ❑ Down–up–down propulsive arm action
- ❑ Body rotating on long axis but head remaining still

Stroke Practices for Advanced Beginners

Arm Recovery Practices

The Periscope Practice

With one hand held by the side (palm down), the other arm is raised to a near vertical position, with the wrist relaxed and the back of the hand uppermost. Good body position is maintained and kicks are strong over a given practice distance (10-25 metres [33 feet to 82 feet]).

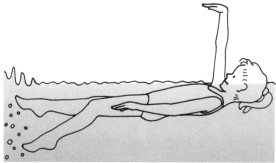

The periscope practice.

Changing Periscope Practice

Raise and lower the arms alternately through 90° to a count of 'right–2–3–left–2–3'.

The periscope practices are designed to develop a vertical movement pattern in the recovery, with the arm reaching up and straight except for a relaxed wrist.

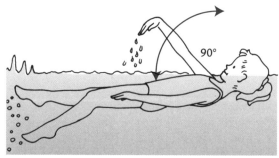

'Let the water drip off your fingers.'

Rotation/Streamlining Practices

As beginners progress they should begin to rotate more on the long axis of the body. The practices in the streamline propulsion section can then be attempted with the body rotating to approximately 70° past the horizontal on each side.

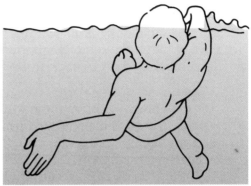

Body rotation on the long axis during backstroke.

Timing Arm Action and Breathing

Once beginners have acquired a sound arm technique, emphasis may be given to the timing of the arm action to the breathing. As one hand enters, beginners take a breath and, while the opposite hand enters, they exhale.

Timing/Streamlining Practices

Gliding Backstroke—Six Count

Beginners hold one arm extended in front and one arm by the side for a count of six kicks, then change position of the arms, with one recovering and entering while the other performs the three sweeps under the water:

'Hold–2–3–4–5–6, change O–V–E–R.'
Check

- body position,
- a smooth changeover,
- kicking technique and
- correct arm movement patterns.

Gliding Backstroke—Three Count

Beginners repeat the preceding exercise to the following count:

'Hold–2–3, change O–V–E–R.'

Measured Backstroke

Evenness of stroke rhythm is the key factor in successful and economic backstroke. Beginners should 'measure out' the strokes by counting 1–2–3 for each arm, where '1' coincides with the entry of the hand.

Evaluating Technique

Teachers should look for the features listed here. The overall timing, or flow, of the stroke is more important than the precision of details.
   Remember, success in backstroke depends on

- smoothness as one arm takes over from the other,
- a high body position in the water,
- balanced movements (right arm is a mirror image of the left),
- maintaining a comfortable but steady head position,
- having a steady, consistent kick and
- pulling, using the bent arm pull and push.

The following backstroke performance criteria have been identified as essential elements of an efficient stroke.

Body and head positions

- Look for the shoulder and upper back rounded towards the breast (slouched).
- The pulling shoulder should sink down almost under the neck.
- Emphasise that there is a slight bend of the body line at the hips. See that the hips are submerged slightly but not sitting.
- Make sure the beginner's chest is at the surface. When the beginner is moving at high speed, emphasise that the torso, from the waist up, is above the surface.
- See that the chin is *not* pressed against the chest or tilted back to see forwards.
- The head should be tilted up about 30°. Watch that the bottoms of the earlobes just skim the surface.

Leg action

- Watch for a steady six-beat kick. It is essential in good backstroke swimming. See that the kick has a moderate bend of the knees (about 30°) and the knees are *not* breaking the surface. See that the direction of the kick is rearwards.

Arm action

- For the arm entry, see that the little-finger side of the hand enters first.
- For the recovery, emphasise that at the end of the pull, the arm lifts out of the water straight and moves over the shoulder. As the arm lifts, so does the shoulder, as if to lift the arm even higher. Beginners can lift the hand little-finger side first and lead with the 'funny-bone' side of the arm, but more advanced swimmers should lift out with the back of the hand.

- For the pull, see that the hand and arm pass through the surface down to a depth of approximately 40 centimetres (1 foot and 4 inches) to catch the water. As the elbow flexes, the palm presses against the water as it moves upwards towards the surface. Emphasise that the arm bend increases as the pull continues and that midway through the pull the elbow points to the bottom of the pool as the arm bends 90°. Finally, see that the hand blades downwards as the arm slowly straightens through the second half of the stroke. Make sure the push ends with a vigorous downwards throwing action. This is called the 'push phase' in backstroke.

Breathing

- Watch for a regular breathing pattern, preferably breathing in on one arm and out on the other.

Stroke timing

- Emphasise that the arms are not opposite to each other in timing. The recovery arm speeds up as it moves to enter well before the pulling arm finishes.

Progressions

Suggested steps

1. Glide and recovery

From a gliding position (shoulders under, head back):

- Horizontal body position
- Head submerged to the crown
- Chin slightly tucked in; recovery to a standing position

It is preferable to teach the recovery first.

2. Glide and kick

- Horizontal body position
- Head submerged to the crown
- Chin slightly tucked in
- Continuous kick without excessive knee bend

Kicking should be practised until it is effective in supporting a streamlined, horizontal body position.

Option

Repeat with arms behind head.

The ability to glide and kick with the arms extended back will greatly improve body position and should be progressively developed, receiving additional attention during the following steps.

3. Glide with kick and arm action

With and without the use of a kickboard:

- Horizontal body position; board held over thighs (fingers on top)
- Simple continuous arm action

Drills with a catch-up to the thigh may become habitual and should be interspersed with practice of an alternating arm action.

4. Whole stroke

Alternating arm action:

- Horizontal body position
- Simple arm action as previously described

5. Breathing

In on one arm and out on the other

6. Stroke refinement

Breaststroke

Following the development of the basic learner sequence, teachers can direct their attention to the teaching of the breaststroke. The breaststroke is an important stroke to teach beginner swimmers because of its survival value. It is also one of the four competitive strokes and has a certain quality which gives swimmers a great deal of pleasure when performing it.

The advantages of the stroke from a survival perspective are that

- the limbs recover under the water,
- a rest or glide phase can be developed to conserve energy,
- the head may be kept clear of the water to allow for a natural breathing style and
- a clear view to the front is obtained.

When teachers teach the breaststroke, beginners should be encouraged to practise appropriate movement patterns to develop symmetrical limb movements. Symmetrical movements conform to the competitive rules of the stroke but, more importantly, maximise the propulsive effect.

The Major Phases of Teaching Breaststroke

Body Position

Beginners should stand with the feet beside each other and slightly apart, the knees bent to allow the shoulders to be under the water. The arms extend forwards in front of the shoulders and the chin rests on the water.

Following a normal breath, the face is placed into the water until approximately one-third of the head is in the water with the face looking forwards and downwards. Beginners push off smoothly to glide.

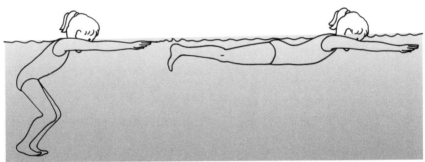

Starting position for breaststroke at the beginner level, before commencing the glide.

During the glide phase the shoulders, buttocks and heels are at the surface of the water with the toes extended in a streamlined position. Adjustments to the head position may be made if the heels do not remain at the surface.

Leg Kick

The kick requires the legs to move simultaneously and in the same horizontal plane.

Kicking Action

Beginners should be given a brief introduction to the actual kicking technique during out-of-water practices. They should lie on a bench or the edge of the pool with the legs extended. The knees

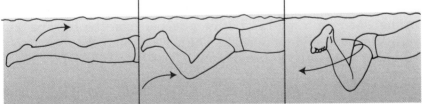

Breaststroke leg and feet actions during recovery and propulsive phases.

bend to draw the heels towards the buttocks. When the knees are fully flexed the feet rotate into the 'hooked' and 'V' position, ready for the propulsive part of the kick. When beginners perform the movement efficiently, practices in water can commence.

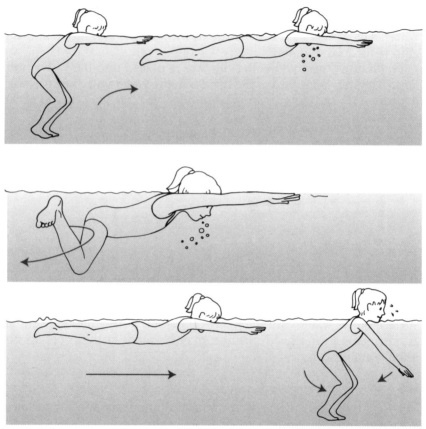

Breaststroke sequence of push off, glide, kick, glide and stand with feet together.

When in water, beginners should stand about waist-deep, with the feet apart and level with each other. They should bend the knees to allow the shoulders to be under the water. Arms should be stretched forwards, shoulder-width apart, with the palms facing the bottom of the water. On a signal, beginners place the face in the water with the head a little deeper than the hairline and push off into a gliding position. During the glide, the feet should assume the inverted 'hooked' and 'V' position. When the glide is performed well, the kicking action can be introduced. The phases of the kicking action should be: push off, glide, kick, glide, stand with feet together.

When one kick can be performed correctly, a sequence of kicks can be linked together: push off, glide, kick, glide, kick, glide, stand with feet together.

Once a sequence of kicks can be performed satisfactorily, the breathing technique can be introduced.

Breathing Technique

As in any swimming stroke, breathing should be as natural as possible. A natural breathing technique implies that swimmers neither hyperventilate nor hold the breath for an extended period of time.

Initial breathing practice should include beginners lowering the face into the water and exhaling through both the mouth and nose while standing. The next stage is to hold a kickboard with the hands apart at the back of the board, fingers on top, thumbs underneath and the arms extended. The kick should be performed with the chin on the water and eyes looking forwards. This practice can be repeated but with the face in the water and exhalation. The face should come clear of the water with the chin touching the water to inhale through the mouth. The face must remain in the water until the kick is completed. When the heels come together, the head should be raised to take a fresh breath.

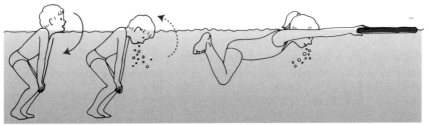

Breathing practice for breaststroke. Breaststroke kicking practice with board.

Arm Action

It is important that the arms move simultaneously and that there is no pushing phase, except during the start and at the turns. The arm action may be divided into three distinct segments:

- Catch and outsweep
- Downsweep and insweep
- Recovery

Catch and outsweep

The arm action commences with the arms fully extended, hands close together approximately 20 centimetres (8 inches) below the surface with the palms turned outwards. The initial movement of the arms is a push outwards until the hands are wider than the shoulders. During this phase of the stroke, the palms of the hands should be applying considerable force on the water. Beginners should be

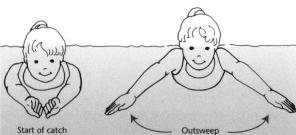

Start of catch   Outsweep

Breaststroke catch and outsweep.

encouraged to keep the elbows locked straight during this phase to enhance the likelihood of symmetrical movements.

Insweep

The lower arms and wrists rotate inwards to enable the palms to face towards the feet as the arms press against the water, while the elbows remain high. When the palms come to a position below the elbows, they sweep inwards to complete the propulsive phase of the stroke.

Arm recovery

Once the pressure on the water has been released from the palms of the hands, the elbows squeeze towards the midline of the body before extending to a fully stretched position, palms downwards.

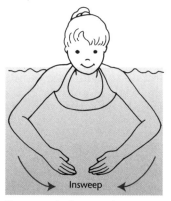

Insweep

Breaststroke insweep in two phases.

As the arms reach full extension, they are pressed down 15 centimetres (6 inches), ready for the commencement of the next stroke. This action keeps the hips from dropping and consequently assists with the maintenance of a streamlined body position.

Beginners do not seem to have a great deal of difficulty in learning the arm action. Beginners can gain initial understanding of the arm action by drawing circular patterns with the hands and arms. If the circular patterns are practised in the water, beginners should stand with one foot in front of the other to provide support and have the shoulders below the surface.

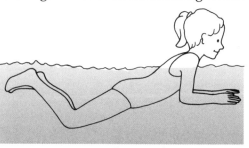

Breaststroke arm recovery.

Breaststroke leg propulsion and arm recovery.

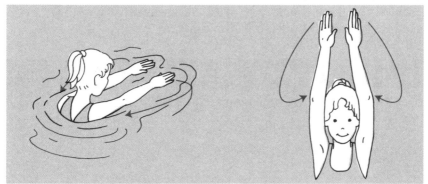

Beginner breaststrokers should watch the hands while practising the stroke to ensure that the hands do not push past the shoulders.

Coordination

The coordination of the breaststroke action varies according to whether the stroke is being performed for survival or for competitive purposes.

Survival breaststroke has a significant glide or resting phase, the purpose of which is to conserve energy. Additionally, it has a slower relative hand and foot speed throughout the stroke.

Competitive breaststroke also has a glide phase, but the speed of the hands and feet is significantly faster, and therefore the glide is shorter.

To obtain an efficient breaststroke technique, it is imperative that the body does not bob up and down as a result of incorrect timing of the leg and arm actions. The correct timing of the stroke occurs when the kick is completed and the arms are fully extended with the body streamlined in the water. At the conclusion of each stroke, whether for survival or competition, the hands-together, legs-together (i.e. streamlined) position must be obtained.

Combining Kick and Arm Stroke

The ultimate sequence is glide–pull–breathe–kick–glide, with the glide being extended for between one and three seconds. Following the push from the wall, beginners should complete an arm stroke and during the stroke lift the head for a breath. This practice may be followed by a kick and a further sequence of glide–pull–breathe–kick–glide.

Beginners feel comfortable with this sequence. Once it has been developed, it does not require relearning or extensive modification—just refinement. Breaststroke, when performed correctly, provides beginners with a relaxed and efficient stroke that can be used in a variety of different situations.

Checklist for Evaluating Beginner Breaststroke

❏ Body is as flat as possible to reduce resistance.

❏ Limb movements are symmetrical.

❏ Leg kick is in the same horizontal plane.

❏ When the knees are fully flexed, the feet rotate into the 'hooked' and 'V' position. (Ankles are dorsiflexed.)

❏ Arms move simultaneously after the glide.

❏ Hands do not push past the shoulders.

❏ Glide action follows the kick.

❏ Breathing is as natural as possible.

Basic Stroke Practices for Beginners

Kicking Practices

- With a kickboard, beginners place their hands apart at the back of the board, fingers on top, thumbs underneath and arms extended. They work on symmetry, ankles flexing and feet turning out on recovery.

- With a kickboard, beginners place the face in the water after a 'normal' breath, push off and glide, then kick and glide and raise the head to the front to breathe after exhaling.

- Beginners try the two previous practices without the board. Beginners have arms extended and shoulder-width apart. They push off and glide, then kick and glide, exhale, raise the head and breathe. They practise a sequence of kicks.

Whole-Stroke Practices

Kick–Kick–Pull

- The aim of kick–kick–pull is that beginners should develop the feeling of driving the body forwards over the hands. The legs should remain together and straight until the *insweep* of the arms is complete and the legs kick as the arms are stretching in front, with the head between them.

Kick–Pull

- The aim of kick–pull is that beginners should improve whole-stroke timing. The arms sweep while the legs glide, and the legs and arms recover as the body moves forwards from the propulsion provided by the arms and previous kicks. The legs sweep before the speed of the body decreases and while the head and arms are streamlined in the front.

Practices for Advanced Beginner Swimmers

Kicking

- Hands trailing behind by the hips, beginners raise the heels on recovery to touch the hands, outsweep, downsweep, insweep, ankles stretch, and glide. Beginners should aim to develop length in the movement pattern and maintain the timing of breathing, leg sweeps and glides.

Gliding Kick

- Beginners count the number of leg movements required to cover a given distance (e.g. 25 metres [82 feet])—'Breathe, leg sweep, glide'. They start the next movement as the body begins to slow down. Ten is a good number for 25 metres (82 feet).

Arm Practices

Pulling

- With a pull-buoy between the legs and with the face in the water, beginners practise the arm movement pattern.

Pulling and breathing

- As in the previous pulling practice, with exhalation on *recovery* and inhalation on *downsweep*.
- With a pull-buoy between the legs and breathing on each stroke (left arm—right arm).

Whole-Stroke Practices

The following practices aim to develop a dolphin-like movement:

- Beginners swim one double-arm stroke and breaststroke kick, followed by two dolphin kicks.
- Beginners swim one double-arm stroke and breaststroke kick, followed by one dolphin kick.
- Beginners swim one double-arm stroke and breaststroke kick, allowing the legs to rise on their glide as though preparing to perform the down-beat of the dolphin kick. The trunk and head should come up and forwards on the *downsweep* of the arms. This style will not suit everyone.

Evaluating Technique

The overall timing, or flow, of the stroke is more important than the precision of the details. Remember, the stroke resembles a series of gentle lifts and lunges forwards, in a snake-like fashion.

The following breaststroke descriptions have been identified as essential elements in an efficient stroke.

Body positions

- Watch for a chain of body positions—with the shoulders rising out of the water, then settling some centimetres below the surface. See that the hips move up and down, but through a shorter range, with the buttocks grazing the surface at the end of each kick.
- Watch that the rise and fall of the shoulders is accomplished by using the muscles of the lower back and not by using the arm pull.
- The sequence of the stroke is important, and the pull, breathe, kick and glide sequence should be consistent.

Head position

- Make sure the head is held relaxed and steady, riding up and down with the shoulders. There should be no separate pumping motions of the head.

Breathing

- Look for inhalation on every stroke when the face lifts clear of the water. Students should exhale through mouth and nose into the water.

Arm action

- In the arm action, watch that when the arms are extended in front they are aimed downwards, with about 20 centimetres (8 inches) of water above the hands.

- See that the pull starts with the hands tilted thumb-side down and the palms facing outwards. The wrists flex first and the arms move slowly apart, with the forearms descending and the upper arms remaining high. The arms sweep outwards until the elbows are in line with the forehead. Then the hands sweep swiftly inwards, followed by the elbows. With that, the final thrust of the hands and forearms is vigorous and aimed slightly downwards, with the elbows about 15 or 20 centimetres (6 to 8 inches) apart. The arm action should not be too wide.

- Watch for an inverted heart shape scribed by the hands during the pull. See that the arm action is continuous, quickening as it progresses. There should be no hesitation while inhaling.

Leg action

- See that the kick is set up with the knees separated slightly more than shoulder width, the lower legs vertical and feet 'floating' just below the surface with toes trailing.

- See that the kick is started by rotating the toes outwards and flexing them towards the shins in a swift, deliberate action. As the feet are swept into the propulsive phase, see that the rearward action is led by the knees.

Progressions

The leg actions for survival backstroke and breaststroke are similar. They differ only with regard to the degree of hip flexion employed, lifesaving backstroke using slightly less.

The initial teaching of breaststroke leg action on the back has proved very effective and is suggested next; thus the development of lifesaving backstroke prior to breaststroke is a possible option. Steps for developing the leg actions for both strokes are similar.

Suggested Steps

1. Foot exercises

Sitting, with legs extended:

- Toes pointed down
- Feet turned out ('hooked' position)

2. Leg action sitting

On edge of pool or similar:

- Thighs unsupported, leaning back
- Knees slightly apart
- Limited hip flexion
- Feet move outside line of knees

Use passive manipulation to direct movement:

- Students push against teacher's hands (pressure on inside of foot).
- Avoid pulling legs through movement.

3. Backward glide and recovery

From a gliding position (shoulders under, head back):

- Horizontal body position
- Head submerged to the crown
- Chin slightly tucked in; recovery to a standing position

Teach the recovery first.

4. Leg action on back

(with board or sculling)
  From a gliding position:

- Glide, single kick, glide initially
- Number of kicks gradually increasing
- Toes turned out before kick
- Shoulders, hips and knees horizontal
- Limited hip flexion
- Glide between kicks

Option

Introduce survival backstroke arm action and coordination. See survival backstroke progressions.

5. Leg action on front

- Land drill
- Lying half in, half out of water
- Supported by forearms in water
  - Toes turn out before the kick.
  - Shoulders, hips and knees are level.
  - Pause between kicks.

6. Glide with kick on front

From a gliding position:

- Glide, single kick plus glide initially
- Arms extended forwards (to board)
- Number of kicks gradually increasing
- Glide between kicks

Exhaling in the water may be included. This will improve body position and assist beginners whose legs sink rapidly.

7. Glide with kick and breathing

From a gliding position:

- Glide with limited number of kicks initially
- Inhaling during recovery of the legs
- Exhaling during the kick and glide
- Whole of face submerged for exhalation

8. Arm action

- Shoulders over lane rope (if safe)
- Lying with shoulders over pool edge
  - Hands press outwards.
  - Hands scull inwards below the chin.
  - Elbows stay high until the end of the inward scull.
  - Pause for the glide phase.

With breathing:

- Inhaling during the inward scull
- Exhaling during forward extension and glide

9. Coordination of whole stroke

One complete stroke

From a gliding position:

- Glide before commencing the stroke.
- Stand after each stroke.
- Make a significant glide with arms extended.
- Exhale during the glide.
- Continue the kick–glide–pull–breathe sequence.

When the water is more than waist-deep it may be necessary to include a kick before the initial glide or to push off from the pool side. If the pool side is used, students should ensure that the glide is gentle or the propulsive effect of the hands will be lost, the arms may pull too far back and coordination will suffer.

Consecutive strokes

The number of strokes should be progressively increased according to success as long as symmetry and coordination can be maintained.

Holding the glide phase for a three-count will assist with promoting the desired timing.

10. Stroke refinement

Butterfly

Following the acquisition of the basic learner sequence of skills, components of the butterfly can be taught. The butterfly stroke is often taught later in the beginner's stroke development as it is perceived to be difficult to master. This is not necessarily the case, and elementary practices of the basic butterfly stroke should be introduced earlier than is the current practice. The learning of the butterfly stroke provides a challenge to beginner swimmers, and many gain a high degree of personal reward from performing the stroke efficiently.

The sequence for introducing the butterfly stroke is similar to that for the other strokes, with the kick being developed following the performance of a streamlined gliding position.

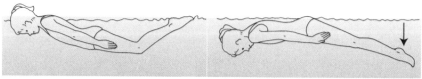

The down-beat of the dolphin kick.

Kick Action

The butterfly kick is often referred to as a dolphin kick and is a powerful action which often affords beginners a great deal of satisfaction. During the kicking action, the legs are close together and move simultaneously.

The kicking action consists of a down-beat and an up-beat performed in a continuous manner. The down-beat commences with the knees bent and the ankles just out of the water. The feet should be pointed and turned in slightly (pigeon-toed). During the down-beat, the legs are forcefully extended or straightened, resulting in a lifting of the hips. On the up-beat the knees bend and the hips go down. Throughout the kicking action it is important for beginners to maintain an undulating body position. The kick must be initiated from the hips and involves the entire body when performed successfully.

Kicking Practices

The following kicking practices are useful for beginners.

'The Man From Atlantis' or 'Aquaman'

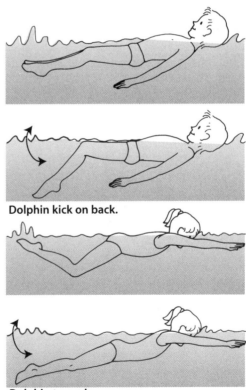

- Beginners submerge, push off from the side, extend the arms in front and dolphin-kick along the bottom of the shallow end for a short distance. Encourage flexibility of hip, knee and ankle joints.

Dolphin kick on back.

Dolphin Kick on Back

- Beginners lie in the back-glide position, with hands trailing in the water. They dolphin-kick, feeling the hips bend and straighten and the water push up from the feet.

Dolphin torpedo.

Dolphin Torpedo

- With arms extended in front
- With hands on hips

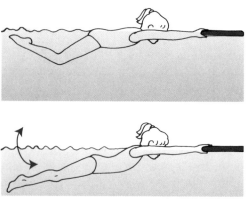

Dolphin Kick With a Kickboard

- With emphasis on the first beat
- With emphasis on the second beat

Dolphin kick with kickboard.

Arm Action

The butterfly stroke is often considered to be the most difficult of the competitive strokes to perform because the arms recover over the water at the same time. Before teaching the butterfly arm action, it is necessary to have a sound understanding of the fundamentals involved.

Entry and Catch

The hands enter the water at shoulder width, with the palms facing outwards to allow the hands to slide smoothly into the water. The hands should submerge to about 20 centimetres (8 inches) below the surface of the water. After entry

- the hands sweep outwards until the hands are wider than the shoulders and
- the palms rotate out during the outsweep until they face back.

The entry is a gentle movement and little propulsion occurs. During the catch, the hands accelerate and provide minimal propulsive force.

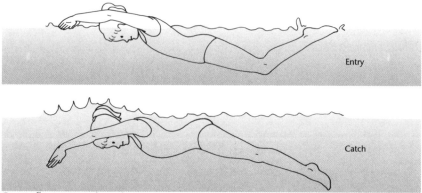

Entry

Catch

Butterfly entry and catch.

The purpose is to 'set the scene' for the propulsive insweep.

Insweep

The insweep is the first of the two propulsive phases of the stroke. During the insweep

- the arms sweep downwards, inwards and upwards in a semi-circular movement until they are under the neck, close to the midline of the body;
- the hands should be pitched to allow the water to be deflected backwards over the palms from the thumb to the little-finger side and
- the hand speed accelerates.

Upsweep

The upsweep is the second of the major propulsive phases of the stroke. The upsweep commences as the hands come close together under the midline of the body. During the upsweep the hand direction changes to a backwards, outwards and upwards movement until the hands come close to the surface beside the thighs, ready for the release. The upsweep is the most powerful and propulsive part of the stroke.

Sequence of the butterfly insweep phase.

Arm Recovery

The release occurs just prior to the arms fully extending and before the hands reach the surface.

- The release is made by turning the palms of the hands inwards to allow the hands to be slid from the water with a minimum of resistance.
- The arms must be extended during the exit from the water to allow a circling up, out and forward movement to occur.
- The arms and hands skim above the surface of the water until the entry is made.
- During the over-water recovery, the palms of the hands should face inwards during the first half and be rotated outwards during the second half.

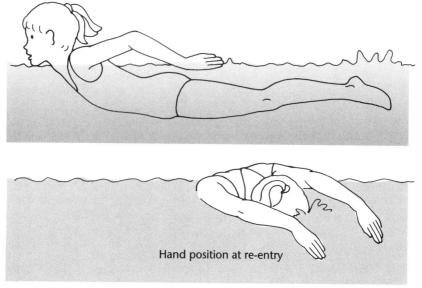

Hand position at re-entry

Arm recovery for butterfly.

Breathing

The breathing action should be as natural as possible, with beginners avoiding excessively deep breathing or holding the breath for too long. During the butterfly stroke, beginners look to the front to inhale through the mouth, as the arms pull. The head should begin to be raised as the arms begin to sweep outwards during the catch. The face breaks the surface of the water during the upsweep of the arms, and a breath is taken and completed during the first half of the recovery. As the arms complete the recovery, the head drops back into the water and exhalation occurs.

Butterfly breathing.

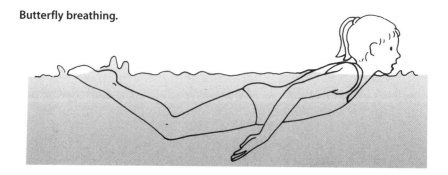

Checklist for Evaluating Beginner Butterfly

❑ Good streamlined body position

❑ Undulating body position throughout the kicking action

❑ Kick initiated from the hips, legs together with simultaneous movement

❑ Kick extended through the legs and ankles

❑ Simultaneous and continuous arm movement (keyhole pattern)

❑ Relaxed arm action on recovery

❑ Breath initiated during the last part of the upsweep

❑ Breath taken and completed during the first half of the recovery

Basic Stroke Practices for Beginners

Arm Action Practices

With the Use of a Pull-Buoy

- One-arm practices.
- Right arm—one stroke.
- Left arm—one stroke.
- Beginners gradually increase the number of strokes from one to six with each arm.

With Dolphin Kick

- One-arm practices as performed with a pull-buoy.

Combination Arm Drills

- One right arm, one both arms and one left arm.
- Two right arm, two both arms and two left arm.
- Any other combination of arm practices may be included as performance improves.

Coordination of the Stroke

One arm stroke, two complete kicks and a breath constitute one stroke. It is considered important for beginners to have a pause between each arm stroke to allow the timing of the arms and legs to synchronise. The glide or rest in the arm action allows the legs to complete the second downward kick.

Evaluating Technique

The overall timing, or flow, of the stroke is more important than the precision of the details. Remember that the butterfly is an involved stroke. All its parts fit together and all are necessary.

Look for the features listed next.

Body position

- Watch for a constantly undulating torso. Beginners should be attempting to poke their buttocks out of the water as the hands enter and glide downwards to a depth of about 20 centimetres (8 inches).

Arm action

- Emphasise an almost continuous arm action, with only a slight pause in front for the catch.
- For the arm entry, see that the arms are loosely extended, with the elbows slightly flexed and pointed upwards. The hands are rotated thumb-side down to about a 45° angle.
- Emphasise that the arm-pull is started by flexing the wrists. Make sure that the arm-pull does not start until the kick has pushed the buttocks to the surface and the shoulders are five or six centimetres (2 or 3 inches) below the surface.
- Make sure the hands are near the surface, out of beginners' line of sight, as the pull begins. See that the pull begins gently, with the forearms descending and the elbows remaining high, just below the surface.
- The pull should not begin until there are five or six centimetres (2 or 3 inches) of water over the shoulders.
- Emphasise that the pull scribes a keyhole or hourglass shape. See that the push ends with the thumbs about even with the leg-line of the swimsuit. Also, at the end of the push, see that the arms rotate from the shoulders to turn the palms inwards.

- Emphasise that the arms are bent at a right angle, the elbows pointing outwards, during most of the pull.
- During the recovery phase of the arm action, see that the arms are not rigid and that the hands are relaxed. The elbows lift out first, followed by the hands.

Leg action

- Watch for the knees bending, leading both the down-beat and the up-beat. The feet and ankles should break the surface of the water before each kick. For the down-beat the knees should be about 15 centimetres (6 inches) apart and the feet should be pigeon-toed.

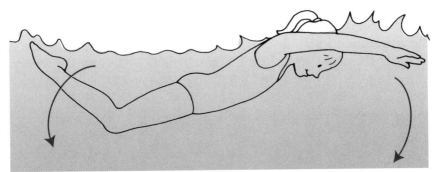

Leg action of butterfly, highlighting the coordination of arms and legs.

- Emphasise a slight pause after each up-beat, with legs high and streamlined.
- Emphasise two kicks per cycle—a kick when the head goes under and a kick when the head comes out. Kick on catch and kick on push (upsweep of hands).
- Check that the hips are high, that the legs are working relatively high in the water and that the head and shoulders are going below with each entry.
- Look for symmetry in the arm and leg movements.

Head position

- Watch for the smooth movements of the head, with the jaw thrust forwards and low.
- For the head–hands timing, see that the head is lifted out before the hands and put back into the water before the hands re-enter the water in front. The head should start to rise when the hands are about a quarter of the way through the underwater stroke.

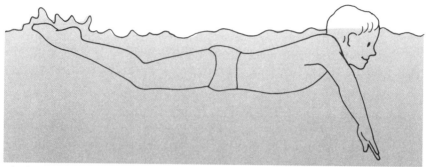

The head rises as the arms complete the first phase of the pull.

Breathing

- Inhalation should be completed during the last half of the push phase and during the first half of the arm recovery. Beginners should breathe out through mouth and nose into the water. Beginners should be encouraged to perform extended breathing on every second stroke or more if comfortable.

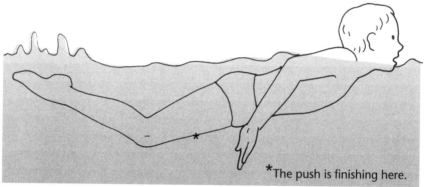

*The push is finishing here.

A breath is taken as the push phase is finishing.

Progressions

Suggested Steps

1. Dolphin kick under water

  a. Arms by sides

  b. Arms extended forwards

- Undulating body

- Head leads movement
- Legs kick together
- Toes turn in
- Lack of excessive knee bend

2. Dolphin kick on surface

On the back:

a. Arms by sides

b. Arms extended forwards

- Emphasis on the up-beat (towards the surface)

On the front:

a. Arms by sides

b. Arms extended forwards

- Emphasis on the down-beat (towards the bottom of the pool)

3. Arm action—without breathing

a. On land (leaning forwards)

b. In water (leaning forwards)

c. Swimming (short repetitions)

- Arms at shoulder width, thumbs down
- Outward press
- Inward pull under chest
- Backward and outward push into recovery
- Back of hand leading wide recovery

4. Combining arm and leg action—without breathing

- Gliding after first kick
- Pushing during second kick
- Short repetitions

5. Combining breathing with arm and leg action

- Head lifting during the press phase
- Face looking forwards for breath
- Face down for the hand entry
- Shoulders remain low

May be repeated, breathing every second stroke.

Option
One-arm drills:

- Breathing to the side initially
- Dolphin kick
- Butterfly arm recovery
- Unused arm extended forwards

May be repeated, breathing every second stroke.

Many combinations may be created using right arm, left arm, double arm, etc.

Option
Whole stroke with extra kick(s) (e.g. two kicks in a glide position before the arm action commences).

6. Whole stroke

- Glide after first kick.
- Push during second kick.

7. Stroke refinement

Sidestroke

Clear vision in direction of travel and uninterrupted breathing are features of this stroke. Each limb action follows a different movement pathway, but as the actions are similar to natural movements encountered in everyday life, the sidestroke is not a difficult stroke to master.

Most beginners will start on a preferred side, but it is desirable that swimmers should be able to perform the sidestroke on both sides.

Body position in the glide is directly on the side with the lower arm extended beyond the head and the upper arm resting along the side of the body.

Leg Action

Sidestroke leg action is called the scissor kick.

The Recovery

From the glide position, the legs bend together to a position where they form a triangle shape with the hips at the apex.

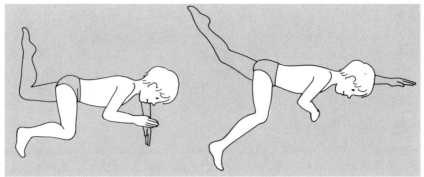

Sidestroke leg recovery. Leg position for the sidestroke propulsive phase.

The legs then separate, with the top leg (i.e. the leg nearest the surface of the water) moving forwards, the knee slightly flexed and the foot dorsiflexed. The action is similar to taking a big forward step.

At the same time, the lower leg is extended backwards, knee slightly flexed and foot plantar flexed (pointed), like a big backward step.

The Kick

From this wide position the feet are swept together in an accelerating circular motion. The foot of the top leg initiates the movement by whipping into plantar flexion as both legs straighten and sweep outwards and around before coming together in the glide position.

The Glide

The swimmer holds the glide position and rests until the forward movement of the body slows, then the next stroke cycle is begun. The glide, or rest phase, is a most important part of this stroke in survival situations, allowing the body to rest and so increase endurance time. During competition, the glide is reduced to maximise time spent on active propulsion.

Sidestroke glide.

Arm Action

In the sidestroke each arm follows a different movement pathway. The action begins from the glide position with the propulsive action of the lower arm and the recovery of the upper arm.

The Lower Arm

Propulsion

The wrist of the lower arm flexes as the hand catches the water; the elbow bends as the hand sweeps in a curved pathway slightly in front of the body line to the shoulder.

Recovery

The lower arm recovers in a spear-like action, extending directly towards the direction of travel while maintaining maximum stream-lining, palm down.

The Upper Arm

Recovery

Propulsive phase of the lower arm; the legs are recovering.

The lower arm recovers as the legs propel the body forward.

The elbow and wrist flex to allow the hand to move up beside the body to a position in front of the lower shoulder where the wrist straightens and the hand extends. Arm and hand remain as close to the body as possible during recovery to max-imise streamlining.

Propulsion

From this bent arm position the hand turns away from the body and pushes in a curved pathway to the thigh, ending in the glide position.

Timing

As the lower arm propels, the upper arm recovers, then continues the propulsive action while the lower arm recovers. This cycle is followed by the glide.

The upper arm provides propulsion to assist the kick while the lower arm recovers.

The upper arm works in conjunction with the legs, both recovering and propelling at the same time. The lower arm works in opposition to this, propelling as the arms and legs recover.

Breathing

Although the face may be held clear of the water, this position increases resistance, so swimmers should master a simple and efficient breathing technique. In sidestroke, the head rests on the lower shoulder with the face under water, and exhalation takes place during the propulsive phase of the upper arm and legs. While gliding, the face is turned upwards, clear of the surface and the breath taken. The head turns back to rest on the shoulder, the face is submerged and the next stroke cycle commences.

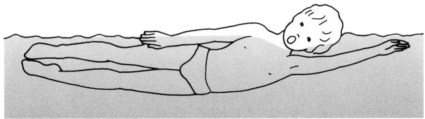

Taking a breath during the sidestroke glide.

Teaching Sidestroke

As beginners sometimes find it difficult to maintain a stable position on the side while floating, it may be helpful to use aids such as kickboards to assist stability when practising leg action.

The Leg Action

After demonstration on land, in the water and perhaps on video, the leg action should be attempted. Key words may help beginners with the sequence.

Bend

Legs remain together and bend to initiate the recovery action.
  Check that

- the legs are together and
- the legs form a triangle.

Open

Legs separate forwards and backwards in giant stride.
  Check that

- their position is wide,
- the knees are slightly flexed,
- the top leg is forwards,
- the top foot is dorsiflexed,
- the lower foot is plantar flexed and
- the movement is in the horizontal plane.

Kick

Legs sweep outwards and around and finish together.
  Check that

- the top foot becomes plantar flexed,
- the kick is circular and accelerating and
- movement stops when the feet meet.

Glide

Legs are straight and are held together.
  Check that

- the legs are straight,
- the toes are pointed and
- the body is directly on the side.

The Arm Action

The arm action may be practised in the water while the beginner walks through the water, leaning slightly sideways towards the direction of travel with the lower shoulder in the water.
Check that

- the arm actions are 'opposite' (i.e. one recovers as the other pulls) and
- the propulsive action has a fluid changeover from the lower arm to the upper arm.

The Inverted Scissor Kick

This is performed when the upper leg moves backwards in the recovery when the legs separate. Turning the swimmer onto the other side may correct this fault initially, but as it is desirable that swimmers perform sidestroke on both sides, it is important that time is spent in perfecting the correct action on both sides. Note: In some rescues the inverted scissor kick may be used to advantage to facilitate towing.

Once the sidestroke is mastered, practices should include

- distance swimming on either side to increase endurance and
- rescue activities—towing a number of partners of different body size and buoyancy, under a range of water and weather conditions, over increasing distances.

Evaluating Technique

Look for the following features:

- The limb actions are smooth and coordinated.
- The body is directly on the side.
- The ear is resting on the lower shoulder.
- The face is angled slightly upwards.
- The arms work in opposite directions.
- The leg action is wide.
- The kick is circular and accelerating.
- The top leg is forwards, foot dorsiflexed.
- Movement is mainly in the horizontal plane.
- The feet meet and remain together for the glide.
- The glide is held for one to two seconds.
- The legs and upper arm work together.

Progressions

It is recommended that the teaching of the sidestroke be left until a symmetrical leg action in breaststroke has been well established. If it is not established, negative transfer of learning may occur, leading to a crooked scissor action during the breaststroke kick. However, the sidestroke has great value in survival and rescue situations and should not be neglected.

Suggested Steps

1. Leg action lying on side

(in very shallow water)
From a position with legs extended:

  a. Bend

- Legs bend together at the hip and knee.
- Bend at hips to 45°

  b. Open

- Upper leg moves forwards, toes back
- Lower leg moves back, toes pointed
- Wide position
- Movement in horizontal plane only

  c. Kick

- Circular, accelerating action
- Toes of upper foot pointed
- Upper and lower legs straighten
- Movement in horizontal plane only
- Movement stops when feet meet

  d. Glide

- Pause for glide phase
- Legs straight and together
- Toes pointed

2. Glide on the side

- Horizontal body position on side
- Ear in water
- Lower arm extended forwards
- Upper arm extended backwards
- Legs together with toes pointed

3. Leg action swimming on side

With board(s):

- Lower arm extended forwards (with board)
- Upper arm extended back (with board)
- Ear in water
- Horizontal body position on side
- Significant glide phase

Option

Add lower arm action to Step 3.

4. Arm action

Standing or leaning sideways in water:

- Lower hand pulling towards shoulder while upper hand recovers towards shoulder.
- Lower arm recovering forwards while upper arm pushes towards the thigh.

5. Coordination of whole stroke

Standing:

- Pulling with the lower arm while the upper arm and upper leg recover
- Kicking and pushing with the upper arm while the lower arm recovers
- Pause for the glide phase

Swimming:

- Horizontal body position on side
- Ear in water
- Arm action, leg action and timing as described previously

6. Stroke refinement

Survival Backstroke

This stroke is an easy stroke to master and is usually taught in conjunction with the breaststroke. As with any symmetrical movements, it is important to emphasise the symmetry, particularly the leg action. There is no vision in the direction of travel, so swimmers should be encouraged to use landmarks as guidelines to direction.

Body Position

Body position is on the back with the body straight and the arms by the sides in the glide position.

Leg Action

The leg action is the inverted whip kick.

The Recovery

From the extended position of the glide, the legs bend at the knees and drop to assume a vertical position with the feet dorsiflexed and averted. The knees are slightly parted but no wider than the swimmer's shoulders.

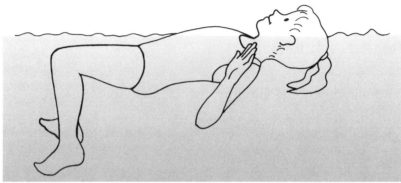

Leg recovery in survival backstroke.

The Kick

The feet are swept in an accelerating circular motion, outwards, backwards and upwards, ending with the feet together, plantar flexed, in the glide position. The movement is symmetrical and simultaneous.

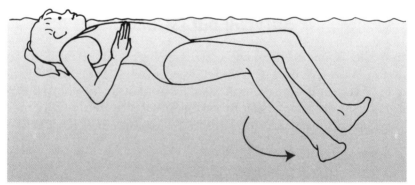

The propulsive phases of the arms and legs in survival backstroke.

The Glide

The swimmer maintains the streamlined glide position until the momentum of the body decreases.

Arm Action

The arm action, like the leg action, is also symmetrical and simultaneous. The propulsive phases of both arms and legs occur at the same time.

The Recovery

From the extended arm position at the side of the body in the glide, the arms bend at the wrist and elbow to allow the hands to move to shoulder level while remaining very close to the body, 'thumbs along the rib cage'. It is important to keep the hands and arms close to the sides of the body to enhance streamlining. When the hands reach shoulder level, they extend beyond the shoulders, elbows bent, with hands facing away from the body and towards the feet.

From this position at the end of recovery the arms follow a curved pathway until the hands and arms reach the glide position.

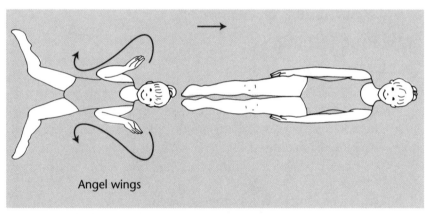

Angel wings

The arm action of survival backstroke—'drawing angel wings'. Arms and legs moving together to complete the glide for survival backstroke.

Breathing

Breathing is natural—usually exhalation occurs with propulsion.

Teaching Survival Backstroke

It is often useful to teach the inverted whip kick with the aid of a kickboard held to the chest to assist buoyancy and to enable the beginner to slow down and concentrate on the correct leg action.

Key words may help the beginner with the sequence.
Bend
Legs bend at the knee and feet dorsiflex.
Check that

- the body is streamlined, on the surface, from the head through to the knees;
- the knees are no more than shoulder-width apart;
- the feet are turned out and
- the body is symmetrical.

Kick
Legs move in a circular pathway.
Check that

- the kick is circular;
- the kick is accelerating;
- the feet finish together, toes pointed, knees straight;
- the knees are under the surface and
- the movement is symmetrical.

Evaluating Technique

Look for the following features:

- The propulsive actions of the arms and the legs are simultaneous.
- The arm recovery begins slightly before that of the legs.
- The body remains symmetrical throughout the whole stroke.
- The glide is sustained.
- The head position is in line with the body with the face clear of the water.
- The knees remain below the surface of the water.
- The combined action of arms and legs provides strong propulsion.

Once survival backstroke has been mastered, swimmers should practise the stroke over increasing distances, while wearing clothes, and while towing people of different size and buoyancy. Multiple rescues should also be practised. These activities should be undertaken under a variety of natural aquatic conditions.

Progressions

The leg actions for survival backstroke and breaststroke are largely identical. They differ only with regard to the degree of hip flexion employed, lifesaving backstroke using slightly less.

Suggested Steps

1. Foot exercises

Sitting, with legs extended:

- Toes point down
- Feet turn out ('hooked' position)

2. Backward glide and recovery

From a gliding position (shoulders under, head back):

- Horizontal body position
- Head submerged to the crown
- Chin slightly tucked in
- Recovery to a standing position

Teach the recovery first.

3. Leg action on back

(with board or sculling)
From a gliding position:

- Glide, single kick, glide initially
- Number of kicks gradually increasing
- Toes turn out before kick
- Shoulders, hips and knees horizontal
- Limited hip flexion
- Glide between kicks

4. Arm action

- Arms recovering close to the body
- Palms pointing outwards (at shoulder level)
- Hands pushing out and down to thighs

Option
Basic arm action:

- Shorter arm recovery
- Simple push to the thigh

5. Whole stroke

From a glide:

- Arms start recovery just before legs
- Arms and legs start push together
- Significant glide phase

6. Stroke refinement